Annie:

You bring me courageous joy.

I am so proud of your strength,
your caring, and your patience.

You are going to "make a difference"
and your faith will carry you
through any doubts.

I love you and I couldn't
ask for a daughter that could
ever "stack up" to you.

Keep your faith strong!

Love,
Dad.

Outrageous Joy

PATSY CLAIRMONT

BARBARA JOHNSON

MARILYN MEBERG

LUCI SWINDOLL

SHEILA WALSH

THELMA WELLS

WITH TRACI MULLINS

Outrageous Joy

The Life-Changing,
Soul-Shaking Truth About God

WOMEN OF FAITH℠

ZondervanPublishingHouse
Grand Rapids, Michigan

A Division of HarperCollinsPublishers

Library of Congress Cataloging-in-Publication Data

Clairmont, Patsy.
    Outrageous joy : the life-changing, soul-shaking truth about God / Patsy
Clairmont . . . [et al.].
       p.   cm.
    ISBN: 0-310-22648-1
    1. Christian women—Religious life.   I. Title.
  BV4527.C533 1999
  242'.643—dc 21   98-55904
                                                  CIP

Scripture quotations are from:

The Amplified Bible, Old Testament copyright © 1965, 1987 by The Zondervan
Corporation;

The Holy Bible, New International Version (NIV), © 1973, 1984 by the International
Bible Society. Used by permission of Zondervan Publishing House;

The King James Version;

The Living Bible (LB), © 1971 by Tyndale House Publishers;

The Message, © 1993, 1994, 1995 by Eugene H. Peterson;

This edition printed on acid-free paper and meets the American National Standards
Institute Z39.48 standard.

Interior design by Jody DeNeef

Interior illustrations by Lyn Boyer-Nelles

Printed in the United States of America

99 00 01 02 03 04 /❖ DC/ 10 9 8 7 6 5 4 3 2 1

Contents

☆Our Divine Ringleader

by LUCI SWINDOLL

In my closet, I have a plaid skirt that's over twenty-five years old, five sizes too small, and quite out of style. Believe me, there's no chance I'll ever wear it again. Not on your life. But will I discard it? Not on your life. My daddy gave it to me.

Anything from him, I plan to keep. Although he's been dead eighteen years, he's still very much alive in my mind. He was a wonderful man: competent, tender, funny, intelligent, and full of wisdom. I thought he was the greatest guy on the planet.

The two of us enjoyed a "mutual admiration society." One year I was trying to decide what to give him for his birthday, and my brothers suggested a framed picture of myself, candles, and matches. "Since he worships you anyway," they reasoned, "he could build a little shrine."

Daddy gave me tangible gifts, and many intangible ones as well. I received letters from him every week when I was away at college, and for years afterward while I worked in another city. The letters were laced with love, encouragement from God's Word, and profound understanding of me—not only as his daughter, but also as a person. He had my best interest at heart and made that very clear, all the time. By his lavish giving, unconditional love, and awareness of my deepest needs, Daddy was all the cheering squad I ever needed. Because of him, I had an excellent model of a gracious, caring heavenly Father.

Although we don't all have that kind of earthly model of love and affection, everybody who is a child of God has a heavenly Father who exceeds all expectations and imagination. My dad may have seemed like the ringleader of our home, but the reason he was such a great parent was he knew the true Ringleader intimately. It was my father's relationship with Christ that made him such a quality person.

Each of us who knows Christ personally can relate to a perfect heavenly Father and become more like him every day. That's incredible! When we become part of God's family, we immediately receive numerous gifts. To name just a few . . .

We're set free from an unrelenting law to experience unmerited grace (Romans 6:14; Galatians 3:25).

We're given immediate access to the throne of God for praise or petition (Hebrews 4:14–16).

We're indwelled by the Spirit of God and guaranteed his presence in all our heartaches and temptations (1 Corinthians 6:19; 2 Corinthians 1:21–22).

We're promised a life that never ends, and a glorious home in heaven (1 John 5:11).

We're given a job to do that has an eternal purpose (Matthew 28:19).

We're forgiven of everything we ever did wrong (Ephesians 1:7; Colossians 1:13–14).

We're assured that all our needs will be met (Philippians 4:19).

We're promised that God will never leave us or forsake us (Psalm 37:25; Hebrews 13:5).

These are only the tip of the iceberg of gifts that become ours. And get this—they're free! All these gifts are given to us simply because we believe what God said, receive what God did, and are now recipients of who God is—the giver of abundant, eternal life.

There is nothing average about the God we know, the Father we long to serve. He's unconventional and exorbitant. He's extravagant in his giving. He's unrestrained in his love for us. In fact, God is extraordinary in every way. He's outrageous! If you and I were to catch even a glimpse of who he is, our lives would never be the same. And yet, he's shown us who he is. His truth and glory are revealed in his Son, Jesus Christ. And we see it every day in the universe he created, in the lives of others, and in our own experience. We often miss it, but it's there. We just forget to notice.

Let's notice. Let's pay careful attention. Let's let our everyday lives be invaded and transformed by this loving, gracious, wonderful, perfectly outrageous God.

The joy he provides is outrageous because it is completely unencumbered by the circumstances we face.

His grace is outrageous as well. It is unmerited, unwarranted, undeserved, and unrelenting. His Word says, "Yet to all who received him, to those who believed in his name, he gave the right to become children of God" (John 1:12).

And peace! The Bible promises, "And the peace of God, which transcends all understanding, will guard your hearts and your minds in Christ Jesus" (Philippians 4:7). Whose life wouldn't be transformed if she experienced that kind of peace no matter what was happening?

And just think about his love. It never ends. It never even waivers. The apostle Paul thrilled at this outrageous thought: "For I am convinced that neither death nor life, neither angels nor demons, neither the present nor the future, nor any powers, neither height nor depth, nor anything else in all creation, will be able to separate us from the love of God that is in Christ Jesus our Lord" (Romans 8:38–39).

And freedom? Now this is fabulous! We have freedom from the law, freedom in Christ, freedom to be all we were created to be. "It is for freedom that Christ has set us free. Stand firm, then, and do not let yourselves be burdened again by a yoke of slavery" (Galatians 5:1).

There's *no* question about God giving us outrageous hope. Hope enables us to feel the intangible, imagine the invisible, and achieve the impossible. We believe God keeps his promises, and with confidence we wait for them to be fulfilled. What God told his people through the prophet Jeremiah is still true for us today: "'For I know the plans I have for you,' declares the LORD, 'plans to prosper you and not to harm you, plans to give you hope and a future'" (Jeremiah 29:11).

God's whole plan to reconcile the human race to himself was outrageous. It was inevitable that his own Son would be outrageous too! Jesus was a man of paradoxes who shocked, surprised, incensed, or delighted everyone he met. As his followers, we shouldn't be surprised that our lives will take some outrageous twists and turns, or that we will sometimes stand out as "circus freaks" in a world that doesn't recognize our glorious nature in Christ. As Thelma puts it, to be a woman of faith means that "your elevator doesn't go to the top floor. Your clock ticks in a counterclockwise direction. Your cart is before the horse. And your joy is always ignited in spite of your delicate condition."

If we really took God at his Word and lived out the implications of these outrageous attributes, our lives would be characterized by what Eugene Peterson calls "the plain meaning of the message of Christ." There would much more than mere moral reformation in us; our lives would be utterly transformed! We'd be like the early Christians whose humdrum human lives became linked to the very life of God himself—the divine Ringleader of the whole shebang. It was then, if you recall, they turned the world upside down.

Grasp the outrageous truth: God is here. God is now. And he longs to pour out all of who he is into your life every day. His life can be in you and flow through you. Outrageous! ☆

Part 1

God's
Outrageous
Love

Five Rings, No Less

by PATSY CLAIRMONT

Ever hear of a five-ring circus? That's what I'd need to feature my wacky, winsome, Women of Faith comrades. These gals are so outrageous, I'd like to spotlight each one—Barbara, Sheila, Luci, Marilyn, and Thelma. They are all clownlike in their joy-giving hilarious ways. Many times they have caused me to giggle myself breathless.

Luci's grandmother, who was obviously a sage, taught her that a day was wasted if you didn't fall over in a heap laughing. Well, I have not only fallen over in a heap at these women's antics, but I've also often been reduced to a Patsy puddle as I've ricocheted from laughter to tears. Believe me, there is nothing like being disabled by a tantrum of giggles. I've learned that moments of unbridled guffawing allow one to release weeks' worth of built-up tension.

Whether we're backstage clowning or onstage sharing, our team is held fast with the glue of good humor and God's love. We have played, prayed, and praised together for the past three years as we've bounded around the country addressing hundreds of thousands of women. What a journey! And what an ongoing joy for me to be under the big top (in arenas) with these caring cutups.

In the pages ahead these multifaceted women will skip, somersault, and twirl through a myriad of topics to encourage and instruct your heart. They will take turns on the tightrope, they'll juggle and swing from the trapeze. You'll notice their versatility as they go from the high wire to the hot dog stand to help you tumble right into truth. So please, come along, and meet the performers the way I would place them if I owned the circus.

First off, we can't have a circus without a ringmaster. (Hmm, or would that be ringmistress?) So I'm pleased to introduce Thelma Wells, outrageous lover of people. I can see her now, sporting a bumblebee whistle and a flashy top hat. Her high energy and persistent interest in people make her a natural to meet and greet the audience. That way Thelma can engulf the folks with her warm hugs and surround them with complete acceptance.

I have never met anyone more genuine or consistent, if not insistent, on caring for and about others. Thelma lavishes love not only on our team members, but her heart also embraces the young, the old, the weak, the strong, the brash, the shy, the striped, and the polka-dotted. Come one, come all under the enormous tent of her heart and find shelter and love.

In the next ring meet Luci Swindoll, outrageous lover of life. She is my candidate for human cannonball. I know she would love the exhilaration of being shot from a cannon to see what new heights she could attain. Luci believes our mission is to investigate and celebrate life—and does she know how to extricate the best out of each moment! Always up for an adventure, Luci travels far and wide exploring this wild and whimsical world we live in.

I love hearing Luci's stories of her escapades from Europe, to Africa, to Antarctica. From her days singing opera, to her visits to museums and castles around the globe, to her balloon safari over the wilds, this woman is amazing. She has demonstrated that complacency is cowardly and risk taking worthwhile. Luci is outrageous! And I love Luci!

The third ring features Sheila Walsh, outrageous lover of freedom. Sheila reminds me of the bicyclist on the high wire. You know, the one who pedals precariously across the thin strand with her head thrown back singing, "La-la-la-la." As if that's not enough, when she nears the halfway point, she stands up on the bicycle seat, balances herself on one high-heeled foot, releases the handlebars, and throws kisses to the crowds.

Sheila sings so sweetly, skims across that high wire so easily, and ministers so unselfishly. It's as if this freedom-bearer can't hold back her enthusiasm. She must share it with others. I just hope I catch a terminal case of her outrageous faith.

Our next ring features Barbara Johnson, outrageous lover of joy. Her joy precedes, follows, and encircles her. She is one world-class juggler. Even in the midst of life's harshest trials, she has kept her plates twirling, her bowling pins whirling, and her hula hoop swirling. When most would have thrown in their juggling balls, Barbara insisted on stepping atop a joy box while adding yet another plate to the rotating stack.

You will want a front row seat to watch Barbara's uncanny display of determination and outright, upright, downright joy. Her entertaining sideshows—stories, quotes, and poems—always liven up the act. She never ceases to amaze the masses (and me) with her dazzling performance during life's dismal predicaments. Her steady eye, hand, and heart make her a phenomenal juggler and an outrageous friend.

Our final ring spotlights Marilyn Meberg, outrageous lover of laughter. Marilyn would make the perfect silver-haired lion tamer. I've never seen anyone she can't mellow out and win over with her contagious laugh, her entertaining wit, and her disarming counsel. Marilyn tames even the snarliest with her winning ways.

Marilyn isn't a whip kind of gal, though. She would much rather win you with a smile—and hers lights up a room. Marilyn's friendly demeanor, her fun ways, and her infectious laughter make her the most amiable lion tamer under the big top. Come one, come all, you're going to have a ball with this outrageous woman!

As for me, I don't want a ring of my own. I'd rather play the clown and bounce into any ring I want. That way I'm less likely to miss out on the fun. Why, I'll light the fuse on Luci's cannon and pull a flower from Thelma's ringmistress's hat when she's not looking. Then I'll wobble on the high wire behind Sheila and stick my head in the lazy lion's mouth after Marilyn's tamed that beast into a mellow fellow. I'll help Barbara juggle a plate or two—till I break one. I figure a clown has a big nose to stick into everyone else's fun and big feet to help her get into ample trouble. And somehow outrageous mischief seems a fitting contribution for me to make to this circus of a life. I love the idea.

You have probably noted by now that our circus sports two words that keep spinning around like cotton candy in the making—*outrageous* and *love*. When you put the two together you have the reason this team exists—the outrageous love of the Lord Jesus. For he brings to us love that can't be measured, emptied, or reasoned. Yes, that's right, God's love is unreasonable. After all, he gave what he loved most, his Son, for those who cared not at all.

Can you imagine that kind of immense, intense love? It is certainly beyond my comprehension. If we placed the three largest illuminated rings available under one big top, we couldn't begin to showcase our God's triune (Father, Son, and Spirit) love for humanity (his incarnation), for us individually (his involvement), and for us reflectively (his indwelling). To us, for us, and in us—that's his gracious and outrageous love.

Glimpsing God's heart makes me want to do back flips while swinging from a trapeze. Trust me, these are not natural feelings for this clown! But then, his is not a natural love. Instead, the Lord's supernatural nature allows us to do things way outside our comfort zone—like love the unlovely, which was what Christ did when he died for us. Now we are called to live lovingly for him.

On that happy and challenging note, let's strike up the band! How about a rousing chorus of "Love Lifted Me"?

Now, ladies, as you tune into the band, why don't you settle into your seats and order your popcorn and drinks? In the following chapters my friends Thelma, Luci, Sheila, Marilyn, and Barbara will amaze and astound you with God's daring feats as they spotlight for you his stunning love. ☆

The Ballyhoo in Bethlehem

by THELMA WELLS

The drums roll as the ringmaster gets ready to make his announcement. "Ladies and gentlemen . . ." The tension rises. "You are about to be dazzled by the most phenomenal event of the evening." Excitement! Applause! Screams of delight!

And the performance begins. The animals and horseback riders and acrobats perform outrageous feats to astound and entertain everyone within eyeshot.

Among the thousands of things that blow my mind about God is that he, of all people, could have dazzled the world with the grandest event of all time. He could have heralded his arrival on earth with the thunderous applause of the angelic host and the clash of a million cymbals. Yet the Almighty, in the person of Jesus Christ, his Son, the Incarnate Word, the Prince of Peace, the Fairest of Ten Thousand, the Lily of the Valley, the Bright Morning Star, the Rose of Sharon, the Wonderful Counselor, the Prince of Peace, came down to earth to live among us in the most ordinary way imaginable.

Just think about it! Mary, Jesus' mother, hid the Savior of the world in her mortal womb for nine months. She probably experienced morning sickness and giggled at her baby's restless kicks. We have no reason to believe that her pregnancy was anything other than ordinary.

And yet this teenage virgin who was engaged to be married became pregnant prior to the wedding ceremony. She never expected God to send an angel to her with such stunning news. It was like being congratulated as the grand prize winner of a contest she had never entered! But Mary did not balk. Rather, she willingly submitted herself to an Almighty overshadowing. And her young fiancé believed her when she told him she'd never slept with a man! Today, if a girl gets pregnant, she becomes the talk of the community or church. Multiply the scandal to the nth degree in Mary's culture! How outrageous that God would select a teenage, unwed girl to be the mother of his Son.

Equally outrageous were the circumstances of that child's birth. You would think, him being the Son of God and all, that during all the months of preparing to welcome the coming King, his earthly parents would have given more thought as to where this baby would be born. You can calculate on nine fingers about what month your baby is going to arrive, so Mary and Joseph knew the child would come during the time they would need to go to Bethlehem to register for the census. You'd think they would have made preparations accordingly.

Now, I realize they didn't have toll-free telephone numbers or the Internet to make reservations at a hotel or the local midwife's house, but you would think that they would know somebody in Bethlehem to stay with, or they could have asked someone going to town on business to make reservations for them at the appointed time. But none of that happened.

They probably thought like some of us: *Well, if we leave early enough we can get there in time to find some place.* Perhaps they did leave early. But a lot of people were going to the same place for the same reason, so the highway was more crowded than they anticipated. By the time they arrived, all the rooms were taken, all the houses were full, and all the tents were at capacity.

Behind one of the inns, the couple found a barn with a stable where the horses, cows, goats, sheep, pigs, and chickens were housed. Now there is no way that I would allow my baby to be born outdoors, let alone in some animal shelter. I'm just proud enough to think my child deserves better. I would have demanded a comfy bed, clean linens, adequate lighting, and a competent healthcare professional. But apparently God's ways are not my ways. He could have snapped his fingers and a greater facility than the Mayo Clinic would have appeared to tend to every need Jesus or his mother might have had. But the almighty God—majestic, regal, royal, sovereign, higher than any mountain, wider than any ocean—chose to make his appearance on earth in a bed of straw.

God's birth in a barn has made a statement to the world ever since: It doesn't matter where you're born or the condition of your surroundings; you can accomplish his ordained purpose for your life.

Before time began, the Father had an extraordinary plan for an ordinary girl: a common virgin would bear God incarnate. My mother was an unwed teenager when she had me. Her mother, my grandmother, was so ashamed of her that she hid her in the house for months. After I was born, my grandmother forced my mother and me to live in servants' quarters in a prestigious section of Dallas. But God had a plan for me, too—an illegitimate black girl, born out of wedlock, in poverty, in the South, in the inner city.

Can anything good come out of illegitimacy and poverty? You'd better believe it, baby! God knew that one day I would be talking to you, sharing his extraordinary plan to redeem and use each and every one of us. In spite of the circumstances of my birth, I was not a mistake. My sainted great-grandmother, who raised me from the time I was two years old, made sure I knew this crucial truth. "Baby," she said, "there was never a seed planted in a mother's womb that God didn't know about and have special plans for. You just remember that. You are somebody!"

I was born in a house on Webb Street in Dallas, delivered by a midwife whose name was Thelma. During the whole nine months my mother carried me, nobody could think of a name for me. In fact, there was absolutely no celebrating when my mother was pregnant. For days after my birth, I had no legal identity. I don't know when I was named, but somewhere along the line I became known as Thelma Louise Smith. When I needed to get a passport in my mid-thirties, however, I discovered that the name I had used for over three decades was not the name on my birth certificate. According to the birth records, my name was Baby Girl Morris.

Morris? Well, my mother's maiden name was Morris, but my father's last name was Smith. Even though I didn't have a relationship with my father, all my life I'd thought my maiden name was his. The only way to legalize the identity I'd always assumed was to go to court and petition for a name change. After presenting school records, affidavits from my mother and other family members, along with additional pieces of proof of identity, I was able to purchase the name Thelma Louise Smith Wells for $175.

I wasn't born in a stable, but I didn't have a legal identity until I was thirty-something. Jesus the God-man was born in a barn, but was positively identified on site as the Savior of the world. Even the cattle in the stalls knew who he was. The sheep and goats, the chickens and pigs recognized the Messiah. The stars shined brighter to point the way to the Christ child. I'm sure some townspeople were drawn to his glory as the angels surrounded the cattle trough with refrains of "Holy, Holy, Holy." Even the straw rejoiced!

God used common folks for the most sacred, esteemed assignment in human history: the birth of his only begotten Son. Jesus' birth was a consummate example of the extraordinary swaddled in the ordinary. And God, in his outrageous love, continues to use ordinary people—you and me—to ring in his kingdom today.

I love the words of the song "Just Ordinary People" made popular by Danniebelle Hall. To paraphrase, it says that God chooses and uses people who are willing to be used by him. Whether what we have seems great or small, God makes it much when we let him have his way in us. He took the loaves and fish from an ordinary little boy and multiplied it to feed over five thousand people. That's what he wants to do with us.

God himself set the example of how to love by living and dying in service to the unlovely. His humble birth into human form—all for the love of humankind—was outrageous! God's very ordinariness is a stunning insult to the proud, a tender delight to the grateful. Every day we are also called to live extraordinary lives in ordinary ways. ☆

Dish Carts and Elephants

by BARBARA JOHNSON

One of my favorite things about Jesus is the way he humbled himself to come to earth and dwell among us. Imagine! He went from the golden streets of heaven to the rugged road of Calvary. If we didn't know it had already happened, it would be outrageous to even consider such a possibility! It would be as unlikely as having the ringmaster step out of the spotlight, replace his tuxedo with work clothes, and join the pitchfork-and-bucket crew that cleans up after the elephants at the end of the circus parade.

When I recently visited the beautiful Precious Moments Chapel in Carthage, Missouri, I was reminded of Jesus' example of humble servanthood. Nestled on the edge of the Ozarks, the chapel features touching murals painted by Precious Moments artist and creator Sam Butcher as his way of showing gratitude for God's goodness. The chapel has become quite a tourist attraction. Since it opened about ten years ago, more than seven million visitors have come from all over the world to see Sam Butcher's tribute to the Lord.

Given all that attention, not to mention the wealth that has come his way as a result of the burgeoning Precious Moments phenomenon, you might be surprised to see Sam Butcher himself scurrying about the visitor center restaurant, greeting guests, listening to guests' stories about why they have come, and pouring coffee. But when he's not working at company headquarters in another state or consulting with one of the company's contractors scattered around the globe, that's the most likely place to find him.

Chapel director Larrene Hagaman told me a wonderful story about Sam's servanthood. It occurred on the third day of the chapel's busiest weekend of the year. Collectors from all over the country had been invited to the chapel and visitors' center to have Sam sign their porcelains and other Precious Moments items. By the end of that third day, Sam's hands were stiff and sore after all those hours of nonstop autographing.

Larrene was hurrying through the guest center on an errand when she passed by the restaurant and noticed the staff was terribly shorthanded. She immediately postponed her errand, grabbed a dish cart, and started clearing tables with the busboys. As she hurriedly pushed the cart into the bustling work area to unload the dishes, she nearly rammed into an apron-clad Sam Butcher.

"What are *you* doing here?" she asked, eyeing the soapsuds clinging to his hands.

He returned her startled look with one of his own. "Well, what are *you* doing here?" he countered.

"They were shorthanded," she answered.

"Well . . ." Sam shrugged as though it were perfectly natural for a millionaire artist and businessman to take the lowest job in the restaurant hierarchy. "Someone's got to do the dishes."

The apostle Paul wrote, "Whatever you do, work at it with all your heart, as working for the Lord, not for men" (Colossians 3:23). In the circus of life, we may relish those opportunities when we can show our love for God by performing in the spotlight. But we really show our servant hearts when we have the same attitude while cleaning up after the elephants! And when we do, God blesses our humble efforts. Sam Butcher learned that fact when he plunged his sore hands into the hot dishwater—and the pain in those tired, aching joints was eased. ☆

The Main Attraction

by MARILYN MEBERG

Recently I visited my two darling grandsons (along with their parents, of course). After an outing in the park, three-year-old Ian made a mad dash for me where I stood waiting by the car.

"Maungya, Mama's boilin' mad ... she's really boilin' mad."

Since I'd never heard him use the expression "boilin' mad" before, I had to swallow my amusement and give him my serious undivided attention. "What's she boilin' mad about?" I inquired.

"Well, I kinda shoved Alec down in the mud [he's one year old and still a bit dottery on his feet] and Mama gets boilin' mad about that stuff."

"Did you mean to shove him down?"

"Yeah. I did it on purpose . . . he was in my way."

"Well, sweetheart, I think Mama has reason to be boilin' mad."

"Maungya, Mama says shoving Alec is not kind. Do you think shoving Alec is not kind even when he's in my way?"

With great conviction I answered that I certainly did think it was not kind to shove Alec no matter how in the way he might be. With a wordless sigh Ian allowed me to buckle him up into his car seat, but he didn't speak to me for several hours.

Before he went to bed that evening, he came out to the living room and crawled into my lap. (I knew he and his mama had been having a heart-to-heart chat.) "Maungya," he whispered into my ear, "I'm gonna try to be kind to Alec."

"That's a good idea," I responded.

He leaned even closer to my ear and whispered, "But mostly, I don't want to." With that admission he slid off my lap and trudged off toward bed. Within seconds he came back to my chair, pulled my ear down to his mouth, and said, "Sometimes Alec makes me boilin' mad!"

I scooped him up and whispered in his ear that sometimes Maungya gets boilin' mad about stuff too. In the interest of time I resisted the impulse to discuss our natural proclivities which veer frequently toward wrongdoing and wrong thinking and that the Bible calls that sin and that it is an inherent condition into which we were all born. After all, it was 9:30 P.M., and Ian is only three.

The amazing thing about God's love is that he can be boilin' mad without losing his love for us even when "mostly we don't want to" do the right thing. He doesn't stop loving us even when we actually do the wrong thing. But God's love is not like cotton candy—sweet, cheap, and easy to digest. It cost him everything, and its demands on us can be hard to swallow. In response to his love, we are called to love as well: love him, love our neighbors, love our enemies—outrageously!

A most outrageous illustration of God's relentless, ever-present, never-going-to-leave-you kind of love is found in the Old Testament book of Hosea. The story opens with God telling the prophet Hosea to go out and get a wife. Sounds good . . . nothing out of the ordinary—until, that is, God describes the kind of wife Hosea is to select: "Go, take to yourself an adulterous wife and children of unfaithfulness" (Hosea 1:2).

How's that for putting you in a spin? What if my son Jeff had come to me for a bit of counsel concerning the criteria he might want to use in selecting his wife. (Actually, I don't think we ever had such a chat . . . amazing . . . he did a fantastic job without me.) And what if I had responded by saying that my one recommendation was that she have a "checkered" past—you know, a tendency toward immorality, adultery . . . maybe even open to eventual prostitution. And if she had not yet shown those tendencies, he would want to note her family background as well as the societal standards (preferably lack of them) with which she was reared so he could be assured that immorality might be her bent. This of course would produce considerable insecurity later for Jeff because after marriage, when the children started to arrive, he'd never know for sure if they were his!

Can you imagine any parent giving that kind of counsel? It's unthinkable. And yet, that's exactly the directive God gave to Hosea.

The outrageously obedient prophet married a woman named Gomer (that name alone would give me pause) who soon became an adulteress and eventually a prostitute. This anguished the heart of Hosea, who had been denounced, abandoned, and replaced by debauched and disgusting men who cared nothing for Gomer. Amazingly, Hosea continued to love her deeply even though he never saw her.

With the passing of time, Gomer lost her good looks and appeal so she was sold by one of her paramours for the price of a defective slave. God, however, was not finished with the relationship he'd ordained for Hosea. "Go," God told the prophet, "show your love to your wife again, though she is loved by another and is an adulteress" (Hosea 3:1). Hosea scouted around until he found Gomer and then, with a broken heart, he bought her back from her current master.

If I were Hosea, I think I'd have one of my worst spells about then! I mean, it would have been like God saying to me, "Marilyn, I want you to take your husband Ken back even though for years he's been unfaithful to you." I can tell you now I'd snort around and probably say to God: "You've got to be kidding! He's the one who left, I didn't! He's the one who's probably populated half the state of California with illegitimate children, I haven't! Not only that, you want me to take him back now that he's bald, potbellied, and spent? He probably has diseases!" With that tirade against God's totally unreasonable directive I might then use my ultimate trump card and remind God I have biblical grounds for never seeing Ken again! Now how could he possibly argue with that?

We have no written evidence that Hosea had the spell I certainly would have had in response to this adulterous scenario (totally fictitious in my case, incidentally!). But God did lay down a few boundaries for Gomer which Hosea was instructed to give her after he brought her home: "You are to live with me many days; you must not be a prostitute or be intimate with any man, and I will live with you" (Hosea 3:3). In other words, Hosea would take her back to his house, but she would have to live in the home she had wrecked with the conscience-stricken memory of what might have been were it not for her unfaithfulness.

That's a powerful, heartrending image isn't it? However, that is not the end of the story, because we ultimately see forgiveness and restoration. God never just leaves his people to dwell in their sinful unworthiness indefinitely. Even his discipline for misbehavior is always within the nurturing, protective environment of his love.

The entire book of Hosea gives us a metaphorical picture of God (Hosea) loving his people (Gomer) in spite of their unfaithfulness. He'd promised Abraham as much when he said he would make of Abe a nation of so many descendants they would be impossible to count. Those descendants came to be known as the Israelites, and there were indeed too many of them to count. But they were an unruly, sin-loving, idol-worshiping, multitudinous gang of rebels who sometimes during the passing of centuries loved and obeyed God but more often than not said, "What the hey . . . let's party!" Though grieved and often angry, God stuck by them. Why? Because he'd promised to never leave them, and God doesn't break his promises, even when we do!

By the time we get to Hosea's story, the Israelites, with their unstable, willful disobedience to God, are at an all-time low. The nation is a mess. They live in civil revolt, anarchy, and bloodshed that has gone on for more than three hundred years. These verses sum it up:

> There is no faithfulness, no love,
> no acknowledgment of God in the land.
> There is only cursing, lying and murder,
> stealing and adultery;
> they break all bounds,
> and bloodshed follows bloodshed. (Hosea 4:1–2)

The homes are corrupt, the courts are corrupt, and even the priests are corrupt. There is no spiritual health to be found.

Into this societal cesspool God drops Hosea to be a prophet to illustrate God's love for his unworthy, faithless bride, the Israelite people. God does this by having the people watch Hosea as he stands by the wayward Gomer, buys her out of slavery, and ultimately brings her home to himself. She didn't deserve that love from Hosea, and neither did the Israelites deserve that love from God. But love he did and love he still does. Why? As my dear friend Alicia Williams says, "He can't help it . . . it's his nature!"

That's not to say that God was not also furious with these people. "Woe to them, because they have strayed from me! Destruction to them, because they have rebelled against me!" (Hosea 7:13). Yet in spite of their godless indifference, sin-seeking preferences, and revolting practices of idolatry, God still said: "I will heal their waywardness and love them freely" (Hosea 14:4).

Now I don't know about you, but that promise is so mind-bogglingly gracious that I could almost volunteer to walk the high wire! God is not saying he'll just look the other way when he sees "waywardness"; he loves us too much not to deal with our rebellious nature. But even when we least deserve it, he loves us without restraint. Outrageous!

Let me take you back a little over thirty years and relate one of my first mother-son conversations about wayward tendencies. Six-year-old Jeff and I were playing with Tonka trucks in his sandbox. He was a bit hard up for companionship that day so when he asked me to join him, I jumped at the offer. Sitting in the sandbox always seemed to produce more vulnerable and transparent musings than sitting around the dinner table.

Jeff and I were making little roads in the sand when, as I'd hoped, he piped up with an interesting tidbit: "Randy's havin' a problem with sin these days." Randy was a sweet little seven-year-old in the neighborhood with whom Jeff sometimes played, but I hadn't seen Randy for a few weeks.

"Really," I said. "I'm sorry to hear that." A long silence followed this comment while I pondered whether I should press for more details about Randy's sin or respect the rights of confidentiality.

"Well, ya see, Mama, he's tellin' a lot of lies . . . I mean a lot!" (Jeff seemed to feel this deeply, so I decided to stay quiet.) "I think he's tellin' more and more lies every day. Sometimes he needs to tell 'em and sometimes he doesn't. But he jist keeps tellin' em no matter what." There was another long pause while Jeff and I switched trucks. "Ya know, Mama, he's startin' to get stomachaches."

Somehow, I felt it wise now to become a more active participant in the conversation. "When does he get these stomachaches?" I asked.

"Well, it's usually right after he tells one of those lies. It doesn't even have to be a big lie . . . he can get a stomachache now with even just a little one!"

"Does he have stomachaches every day?" I asked casually.

"Yup," Jeff said. "He's decided to quit snitchin' Mystic Mint cookies . . . he thinks maybe that might help his stomachaches a little."

After another pondering silence Jeff asked if I thought God was mad at Randy or had God maybe not noticed the lies . . . and if he had noticed the lies would God quit loving Randy? I assured Jeff that God would not stop loving Randy in spite of his "sin problem," but that God would really like to help him with the lying.

Jeff stopped dead in his truck tracks and stared at me. "But what can God do about it? God's not doin' the lyin, I am . . . I mean . . ."

"It's okay, Jeff, I had a feeling we weren't talking about Randy's tummy."

That night as Jeff and I were going through our bedtime ritual, he prayed for forgiveness and asked God to help him not lie "even when it seemed smarter to lie."

I was so delighted to see my son learning values, so eager to assure him of God's dependable love while also teaching him that "waywardness" is something God means to redirect and heal. God loves us too much to leave us muddling about in our sin. No matter what our problem—lying, cheating, marital unfaithfulness, yelling at the kids, fudging on the income tax, bitterness, anger, gossip, etc., etc.—God is tenacious in his commitment to developing us into people of integrity who love him, reflect him to others, and delight in doing his will.

In the midst of our stumbling, wayward humanity, God "loves us freely." Abundantly. Outrageously. Not even the Gomer inside each of us can resist an attraction like that! ☆

I Love You Anyway
by BARBARA JOHNSON

Lord, how can you love me,
Odd as I am?
Rattled and railing and flailing my hands?
How can you claim me, Lord,
Weary and worn,
Beaten, defeated, belittled, and scorned?
How can you need me, Lord,
Helpless and frail,
Senile, demented, frightened, and pale?
How could you die for me,
Worthless and stained,
Arrogant, sinful, thoughtless, and vain?
How, Lord—
How could you? . . .
What?
What's that you say?
Not because, child—in spite of.
I love you anyway.

Ann Luna

Chapter 3

The Performance Is Finished

by SHEILA WALSH

"Worth it all." I believe those would be the words of Job if he sat down with Diane Sawyer for a face-to-face interview on "A Sinner in the Hands of God." A skeptical world would doubt his sanity. Remember his story? We read in the Old Testament that he was quite a man. In fact, God said, "There is no one on earth like him." Quite a reference! Of all the people in the world, Job pleased God the most.

But then Satan approached God and said, "The only reason Job loves you is because you bless him. He has it made. If you took your wall of protection away, he'd curse you to your face."

God knows better, however, and lets Satan have his way with Job . . . for a time. "Have at him," God says. "You can't take his life, but anything else is fair game."

That's mind-blowing to me—not only that God would let his enemy go after his most righteous child, but that Job still loves God after it's all over. I mean, what kind of person puts their trust in a God who stands back and lets hell blow in his face? That's outrageous!

Diane Sawyer questions and probes, trying to make sense of what is senseless to her. Job's bottom line: "I'd heard about him before. Now I know him. Not from far off, but right here," he says, pointing to his heart.

Diane is silent. There is something bigger here than she even imagined. She can see it in his eyes. Not the wild ravings of a misguided fanatic, but something outrageous nevertheless.

I love the outrageous. There is something about the shock to my system of being surprised that shakes me out of my lethargy and makes me think . . . whether I like what is being said or not.

There's no question that God is outrageous. Just think about it for a moment. Try to put your tiny feet into the gargantuan shoes of the Deity. First of all, into your perfect world . . . oops! I'm going to have to back up already. It wasn't perfect. There was Lucifer. Beautiful angel. Trusted angel who looked at God's shoes, then at his own feet, and thought, "I think we're about the same size." Well, he was wrong, and his rebellion bought him a ticket straight out of heaven. Like all rebels, he took a lot of others with him. That had to have broken God's heart. He had given Lucifer a position of power over other angels, and instead of rising to the occasion, Lucifer sank to an all-time low.

I would think that at that point God would have thought, *Okay, bad idea. No more choice. No more sharing my life, my power with anyone.* But that's not what God decided—which is why I say that God is about as outrageous as life gets. What he did instead boggles the mind: he created Adam and Eve. Hello! Rather than making him more cautious with his gifts, God's experience with Lucifer led him to make beings in his own image and give them free rein over all of creation.

I don't think it's possible to imagine what that garden life was like for Adam and Eve. Before the world fell, there was no discord, no dissatisfaction, no "bad days" or PMS. So often I blame my bad behavior or attitudes on the time-of-the-month or "I didn't sleep well last night," but for Adam and Eve there were no excuses. They had it all. And yet they still said, "I wonder . . . ?"

When I was a child and I got stung by a bee or a zit exploded on my face, I would mutter under my breath, indicting Eve for throwing open the door to every petty ill that clouded my small world. Now as I have eased into my forties, I'm convinced I would have fallen as fast and as hard as she did because I'm no different from her. Each one of us has the same bent toward rebellion. And yet knowing that, knowing all of that, God made us. Why? It makes no sense to me.

Cast your eyes back over the past few centuries of human history. If you were God and you knew what we were capable of . . . the hatred, jealousy, infidelity, child abuse, murder, war . . . would you have gone ahead with your plan for the world, or abandoned the whole human race idea? In my limited understanding, I definitely would have said, "Forget it, this will never work. No good can come of it."

But that's not what God said. He laid all of heaven and earth at our feet, even his own Son. As a mom of a two-year-old, I know this kind of giving is beyond me. It's outrageous! So why? Do you ever ask yourself, "Why did God make me?" It reminds me of a joke I heard.

One day while Jesus was walking around heaven, he saw an old man sitting on a cloud, weeping. Walking over to him, Jesus asked if he might join him.

"I'd be glad of your company," the old man replied.

"I was wondering why you are crying," Jesus said. "This is a place of joy . . . no more tears, no more sorrow."

"I was thinking about my son," the man confessed.

"Tell me about him," Jesus said.

"Well, when I was on earth I was a carpenter and I had one son. He was different from all his friends . . . no one quite understood him." The old man paused for a moment, caught up in another time.

"Different?" Jesus asked.

"Yes, quite different," the man replied. "He followed in my footsteps. He became a carpenter, too, and he brought nothing but joy to my heart. He was a wonderful boy, but he was eventually betrayed by those he counted as friends." Fresh tears coursed down the old man's cheeks. "I just wish," he continued, "that I could look into his eyes once more and tell him how much I love him."

Jesus looked closely at the old man for a few moments. "Papa?" he whispered.

"Pinocchio?" Geppetto replied.

Bad joke, I know. Funny, but bad—I just hope my mom doesn't read this. But before you write me off as an irreverent heathen, consider this: What were God's motives for making us? In the Pinocchio story, Geppetto carved the puppet out of wood so he could travel around the country with him and make a living with this dancing spectacle. Is that why we were created . . . to entertain a bored Deity? Was time hanging heavy on the Almighty's hands? Or was God a tyrant who created those he could then rule over? Perhaps we are the recipients of a magnanimous power who was searching for a place to pour an excess of warmth and affection. Or is he a good God who simply wants obedience from loyal followers who choose to serve?

He is certainly the latter, but is there more? If we weren't made to dangle like puppets or serve God from a distance or work for a noble cause until we drop, then what? I'm learning a lot about God's character from my little boy.

It had just stopped raining when Christian and I walked across the mall parking lot to the car. Now the sun was shining, causing steam to rise from the sticky asphalt. A hundred yards from our car was a large puddle. We walked up to it and stopped at the edge. Christian looked at me and I looked at him and then at our white summer shoes. As one soul we both jumped into the puddle at the same time and splashed and splashed until little drops of water ran down our legs and onto our now muddy shoes.

That's how the outrageous message of the love of God affects me. You see, experiencing God's love and loving him in return is not just about living a good life. It's not just about duty or obedience. It's about loving with abandon. It's knowing he's still there when everyone else has left. Job got it. He would have joined us in the puddle.

Remember these wonderful words from Romans 5:1–5: "Therefore, since we have been justified through faith, we have peace with God through our Lord Jesus Christ, through whom we have gained access by faith into this grace in which we now stand. And we rejoice in the hope of the glory of God. Not only so, but we also rejoice in our sufferings, because we know that suffering produces perseverance; perseverance, character; and character, hope. And hope does not disappoint us, because God has poured out his love into our hearts by the Holy Spirit, whom he has given us."

You say, "Not me. There's too much I've done, am doing." I understand. I spent so much of my life trying to make God glad that he had chosen me. I walked a very narrow tightrope for years, afraid that I would fall off and disappoint him. When I look back at my teenage years and into my twenties and thirties, I'm glad that I didn't sleep around or mess with drugs. I don't regret the fact that I didn't rebel, I just wish I'd enjoyed the journey a bit more, that my choices had been rooted in love and not in fear. I thought I understood Christ's words from the cross as he cried out, "It is finished!" But I didn't.

Now as I look into the eyes of my son I have a whole new understanding of the heart of God. There are days when Christian is a pure delight, and other days when he's swinging the cat by the tail and putting my new pale blue suede pumps down the toilet. But on those soggy days I don't love him any less.

My love for my child is only a pale reflection of God's love for you and me. Perhaps you had a mother or father who made you feel every day of your life that you had to prove yourself, and so you have no human model to even begin to grasp the ridiculous love of God towards you. I wish I could sit down with you face-to-face, listen to whatever you might have to tell me about your life, and assure you . . .

God loves you. Not as a puppet or a scalp hunter for Jesus, but just for you. God loves you and made you for the pleasure of knowing you.

Sit with that for just a moment. Isn't it outrageous? Then imagine with me that a movie was made of your life. Nothing was left out. Everything you've ever said or done was right up there on the big screen for everyone to see. How would you feel? Ney Bailey, a dear friend of Women of Faith, asked us that once. And then she reminded us that the great outrageous news of the gospel is that God has seen our movie, the whole story, and he loves us.

Let me say that one more time in case you missed it: God has seen your movie—the whole story of your whole life—and he loves you. No matter what. Even if you feel that there is something in your past or present that negates the grace of God, there is no such thing. All you have to do is be willing to receive.

> Here is love vast as the ocean
> Lovingkindness as the flood
> When the Prince of Life for ransom
> Shed for us his precious blood.
>
> Who his love will not remember?
> Who can cease to sing his praise?
> He will never be forgotten
> Throughout heaven's eternal days.

Doesn't that make you want to sing! I have an even better idea. Get on your best white shoes, find the biggest puddle you can, and give me a call. Christian and I will be right over, and with every splash of water we'll celebrate the outrageous love of God. ☆

Barbara's ABCs of Outrageous Love
by BARBARA JOHNSON

Love . . .
  Accepts,
  Believes,
  Caresses,
  Dreams,
  Embraces.
Love . . .
  Frees,
  Grows,
  Heals,
  Invigorates,
  Justifies,
  Knows.
Love . . .
  Lasts,
  Matters,
  Nurtures,
  Overlooks.

Love . . .
  Protects,
  Quickens,
  Relieves,
  Serves.
Love . . .
  Tries,
  Unites,
  Values,
  Warms.
Love . . .
  eXcites,
  Yields,
  Zealously defends.
Outrageous!

Part 2

God's Outrageous Grace

Skipping Across the High Wire

by PATSY CLAIRMONT

This clown is not wild about heights. No, not me; I'm a true landlubber. Just nail my baggy pants, flouncy hat, and floppy shoes to the earth, thank you. Once on a whim (or was it a hot flash?) I climbed up a lifeguard's lookout (he wasn't there), only to freeze when I attempted to return to good old terra firma. A friend eventually coaxed me down one baby step at a time. So you can imagine how scary life has seemed to me when my personal path has narrowed to a threadbare wire, my options have thinned out, and no signs of help have been visible on the horizon.

Help is what we girls, Barbara, Thelma, Marilyn, Luci, and I, often have thought we would need to offer high-wire Sheila. If you've attended a Women of Faith conference, you know Sheila wears the most outrageous high-heeled shoes. If their vivid colors don't catch your eye, I guarantee the outlandish height of the heels will. How high are they? Well, let's just say I climbed into them one day, and my ears began to pop and I developed a nosebleed.

To make matters even more knee-knocking for us teammates, Sheila often walks—sometimes even skips—in these heels to the extreme edge of the platform while speaking, allowing the toes of her shoes to hang off the stage. Luci,

Marilyn, Thelma, Barbara, and I, who are seated five steps below the platform, gasp as we go into full-body alert, ready to throw ourselves forward if she should topple. That hasn't happened . . . yet. But we are willing to respond if our daring, high-wire cohort should need our help.

Isn't that a tiny picture of what grace is all about? The Lord is there for us when we need him most and possibly deserve his involvement least. Yet grace is more, for it isn't limited to unexpected slips on the high wire; it also encompasses those times when we think we can't take the next scary step. Then he gives us the grace to let go of the pole and inch forward in baby increments, or sometimes even skip like a gazelle.

Grace is undeserved and full of mercy, compassion, and generosity. It's such a divine concept, I believe we finite beings have trouble embracing it. For us, the grace concept is like a balloon on a string dangling just beyond our grasp.

As unbelievable as it seems, grace is full of forgiveness and overlooks faultiness and frailty. Our human tendency is to keep detailed records of each other's errors and even find satisfaction in reciting the weaknesses of our sisters and brothers. We tend to hoard our niceness and dole it out in small increments to a chosen few. The grace of God, on the other hand, generously extends itself. We lean toward being selective lovers, while God is an extravagant lover, receiving us with open arms, seemingly blind to our ragged, wretched condition.

Grace is powerfully exemplified in the story of the Prodigal Son. The prodigal had been unruly, disrespectful, and self-serving. Yet when he fell off his high wire (or as my dad would have said, his high horse), he repented and returned home. Upon his arrival his daddy—get this—runs to meet the returning, wayward, clown of a son and greets him, not with accusations, but with grace-filled relief and acceptance.

That portrayal deeply moves me. Actually, it makes this clown cry. Perhaps because I was a runaway teenager, and when I returned home, my mom ran to extend grace to me. The prodigal and I know how undeserving we were.

I need continuing grace in my life today. In fact, I long for it. For in grace's company, I feel humbly clean, fully accepted, and totally safe. But I must confess I'm a novice grace-giver, which is why I can't wait to climb under the big top with my friends Barbara, Luci, Marilyn, and Sheila to hear their insights on this mysterious, holy quality of Christ's. In the following chapters, they will help us take hold of the balloon's string and draw down grace that we might understand it better and extend it to others.

Grace. What an outrageous concept! Hooray, even clowns are invited! Come, skip along with me, and grasp grace for yourself. ☆

Chapter 4

Spinning Plates, Juggling Melons, and Singing the "Hallelujah Chorus"

by SHEILA WALSH

A raw deal. That's how it always seemed to me. There's Mary, sitting at the feet of Jesus as if beds make themselves and dinners fly out of the oven spontaneously. She gets to be Mary because Martha is willing to be Martha. If Martha sat down, they would all be hungry and the house would be a mess and no one would be feeling very blessed. Martha runs herself ragged doing everything for everyone, but no one appreciates her; no one notices her selfless efforts.

57

Sound familiar? It does to me. There are days like today when I feel I'm about ten minutes away from crawling under the bed with a large box of chocolate chip cookies and never coming out again. In my mind's eye I can see it all. I'll take a couple of pillows and a blanket, a portable television, but no phone—definitely no phone. I'll hear my husband calling for me, but I'll stay really quiet knowing he'll never think to look under the bed. The cats may wander in every now and then, but seeing I'm unwilling to share the cookies, they'll leave!

Do you ever feel that way? You know that if one more person asks you to do one more thing, you'll end up on the six o'clock news: "Local woman turns into mad terrorist, assaulting neighbors with large jar of pickles."

Life just seems so much more complicated than it used to be. Even the stores add to our stress. When I was a young girl growing up in Scotland my mom would send me to Mrs. Skelton's, our corner grocery store, for any last-minute forgotten items we needed for our evening meal. It was a small store, about the size of an average guest bedroom, and I could stand in one spot and see everything she had. I could be in and out in two minutes.

Not now. The other evening I realized that I was short of pasta for our spaghetti dinner, so I grabbed my purse and shouted up the stairs to my husband Barry, "I'll be back in a minute, I just need something from the store." Two hours later I wandered in, shell-shocked.

"Where on earth did you get to?" he asked.

I stood, mute, an inane grin on my flushed face. He continued, "The spaghetti sauce is like a burnt offering, the baby's in college, and the cats have become missionaries to China!"

I tried to reconstruct how it had all happened. "Well . . . I was looking for pasta but I couldn't find that aisle but I found a new kind of cat litter for households with more than one cat. There was a scoopable litter for three or more cats with a cold or a nonscoop for two cats and a ferret, just nothing for two regular cats. Then I realized that we needed cereal but I couldn't remember if you like Fruity Bee Bops or Boppie Fruit Pops. I saw the toothpaste aisle, but do you want white, white teeth and rotten gums or healthy gums and teeth like a rodent? When I finally staggered back to the car, I remembered we needed pasta!"

Can you relate? Perhaps you're the only one with the initiative to plan Bible studies or fellowship events, but underneath it all you're so mad that no one appreciates what you do that you're contemplating slipping some Ex-Lax into your friends' cookies. A familiar communal wail goes up from churches all around the world: "It's the same people who do all the work all the time!"

Barry and I hit this wall a year into our marriage. We looked at our strengths and decided that I was better with money, so I'd pay the bills and balance the checkbook (when I say balance, I mean get it to the closest twenty dollars!). Things were fine for a while, until I started getting busier. I remember sitting on the floor one night close to midnight, writing bills, and getting madder and madder by the moment. When I finally got to bed Barry asked me, "Are you all right, honey? You seem kind of quiet."

"I'm-just-fine-thank-you-very-much," I replied with all the warmth of a terrorist.

"Whoa there, I think I missed an episode somewhere."

"Oh, just go to sleep—I'm sure you need your rest, you poor exhausted little thing."

Then he made that fatal male mistake. "Is this a bad time of the month?" he inquired innocently.

Razzle fazzle, razzle fazzle!

The next day I went to see a friend of mine who is a wonderful and wise counselor. "What's up, Sheila?" he asked. "You look like you're about to give birth to an Indian elephant."

"I'm just so mad at Barry!" I wailed.

"Why?"

"Well, I'm really busy with writing a book and all sorts of things, and yet I'm still paying all the bills and taking care of our checkbooks."

"Then why not give that task over to Barry," he suggested.

I looked at him as if he'd just advised me to hire a giraffe to do the ironing. "What if he doesn't do a very good job?" I said.

"You know what your problem is, Sheila?" he asked.

"What?" I answered quietly, hoping he didn't hear me and therefore wouldn't tell me.

"You like to be in control."

"I thought that was a spiritual gift!" I replied, wondering if I could ease my way out of the building before he noticed I was gone.

"You have two good choices here and one really bad one," he continued, ignoring my irreverent attempt to sanctify my character defects. "You can carry on doing what you're doing but with a good heart, taking your strength from the grace of God daily. Or you can ask Barry to take this responsibility from you and tell him it's too much for you now."

"And what would my bad choice be?" I asked, not thrilled with one or two.

"Doing what you're doing right now!"

Drat! I knew he'd hit on that simple truth that the only person in life I get to choose for is me. I can't change Barry or Christian or anyone else (trust me, I've tried). But I can choose how I live, how I react. I can't blame my bad behavior on anyone else but me. I hate that!

So I went home and asked Barry to forgive me for my rotten attitude. I told him that I was feeling overwhelmed and asked if he would take over paying the bills and balancing the checkbook. He took it over that day, and it was such a load off my mind. Now he can balance the checkbook to within a dollar. I didn't even know that was possible!

So much of life is going, going, going, and doing, doing, doing. But we don't have to do everything ourselves. We can ask for help . . . if we're willing to let go of our demand to be in control and our desire to impress others (even God?) with our superhuman efforts.

How do we ever find balance in the midst of all the demands that are placed on us? As if that's not tough enough, add in the question, "What does God expect of me?" The answer is one that I think we often get very wrong. What's wrong with the picture I drew of Jesus' friend Martha? To me, it's simple. Martha had no joy in being Martha. She kept busy "serving," but she hated it and resented what she "had" to do.

Tony Hancock was one of my favorite British comedians before his untimely death. He began his career with a series of radio plays and then moved to television. As a child I watched on our little black-and-white TV as he fought his way through a barrage of impossible situations.

One episode stands out in my mind. In an outburst of goodwill to all men, Tony decides to donate blood to the Red Cross. I can still picture him sitting in the waiting room, feeling decidedly saintly. He asks the man beside him if they get a badge for their selfless act. "Nothing flashy," he insists. "Just something like . . . 'he gaveth so that others might live.'"

He is visibly deflated to learn that such a vulgar token is not offered. He then wonders how much a pint of blood is worth, as he likes to keep a record of all his good deeds, with price tags attached, in a notebook. But no one is willing to price his corpuscles. He finally takes comfort in the fact that when he is called to face his Maker he can simply hand over the notebook and say, "There you are, mate, add that lot up!"

Tony missed the point. It's not about what we can do for God, but what his grace is doing in us. I still laugh when I see old reruns of "The Blood Donor," but I wonder how far away you and I are from Tony's misguided attempt to win God's favor.

So how do we continue to make good choices and enjoy God's grace in the midst of tough times? Well, first we have to make a habit of drinking deeply of the grace God promises, every moment. The apostle Paul knew the secret: "But he said to me, 'My grace is sufficient for you, for my power is made perfect in weakness.' Therefore I will boast all the more gladly about my weaknesses, so that Christ's power may rest on me. That is why, for Christ's sake, I delight in weaknesses, in insults, in hardships, in persecutions, in difficulties. For when I am weak, then I am strong" (2 Corinthians 12:9–10).

God's grace is here, now. We just have to uncover our soul and let grace soak us to our roots.

Second, we have to keep our sense of humor. I find it helpful to have a few things up my sleeve for those tougher-than-usual days when the melons are landing on my head. It's like a survival kit for my personal moments of madness. I have several funny videos that just knock me over. I've taped a few of my favorite *All in the Family* episodes. I have a copy of a letter that an Egyptian friend of my mother's wrote to her where the choice of words is all wrong and so funny. My box of special photographs of my friends and family always cheers me up. So does getting out into the fresh air and walking across the field to watch my neighbor's horses. Christian and I lie on our backs on the grass and wait for the moon to come out. Sometimes I read one of my favorite Psalms (see, if you hang around long enough I will do something really spiritual!).

God is all around us, longing to talk to us, to love us, to lift us up. Make up your own survival kit. Find things that you know can lift you above the hubbub in your house and in your head.

The wonderful and outrageous thing about grace is that you get to be Mary or Martha, and if you really understand grace, both bring joy. You can be Martha, getting things ready for everyone else to enjoy—loving every minute of it because you're doing it for God with real joy in your heart, not just a fixed grin on your face as you silently smolder. You surrender the need to be noticed, to be appreciated. You take your eyes off everyone else and live your life, share your gifts.

Or you can be Mary and slow down for a while and sit at Jesus' feet, surrendering the desire to always be in control and valued by what you do. That was one of the hardest lessons for me to learn. I thought that what I did for God and others made me loved, but I was really fed up with it. Now I understand that I am loved by God anyway, even if I do stay under the bed for a couple of months. So I enjoy most of my busy days, and when I get a day like today I make a cup of tea, sit down with Christian, and watch the Barney movie for the nine hundredth time.

You see, when you really "get it," really understand that God's grace is enough and will always be there, then you can spin plates, juggle melons, and sing the "Hallelujah Chorus"—all four parts, all at the same time. And you'll be sure that God's grace is sufficient even if a few of those melons splatter on the ground! ☆

Grace for the Bewildered
by BARBARA JOHNSON

Recently I saw a silly cartoon that depicted a stout little bearded fellow wearing a biblical-era robe and smiling in the midst of two giraffes, two dogs, two elephants, two snakes, and several other pairs of creatures. The little man and his animals were gathered around a big sign near a gate that said, "Noah's Park." The voice coming down from above said something like, "Okay, now, let's try it again. And this time, listen carefully!"

Thank heaven Noah didn't really misunderstand God's instructions, even if he was six hundred years old! If only the rest of us had such spiritual acuity. Sometimes, feeling pressured, I think God is telling me, "No!" and I hesitate to act. Then later, when things have settled down, I decide he was probably saying, "Go!" Other times I waffle, wondering whether he wants me to "Hop" or "Stop," "Learn" or "Turn."

How wonderful it is when God's intentions come through loud and clear and we can respond appropriately. We aren't confused like the old woman who was interviewed by a young reporter on her 102nd birthday. As he left, the reporter said to her, "Who knows? Maybe I'll see you again next year."

"I don't see why not," the old woman replied. "Looks to me like you're in pretty good health."

There are times when God's will isn't obvious to us. Do we stay in this job or accept another offer? Do we join the big church on the corner or the newly formed store-front congregation? Should we enroll our kids in public school or private? How do we decide which choice God wants us to make?

The Bible says Noah "walked with God" (Genesis 6:9). It doesn't say he *talked* with God. Instead the image implies quiet companionship. Noah walked with God—and, no doubt, he listened. He "found favor in the eyes of the LORD" (Genesis 6:8). Noah spent time with the Father, and during their time together God spoke to him. And as outrageous as God's instructions may have seemed at the time, Noah set about building an ark. He stepped out with courage to do what he perceived as God's will. And later, if Noah had learned that God had been telling him to build a "park" instead of an "ark," he would have asked forgiveness and started over. For Noah served the same God we serve, a great God of grace. ☆

Chapter 5

A Ticket to Ride

by MARILYN MEBERG

Patsy mentioned the story of the Prodigal Son . . . the one who took off with his inheritance, stupidly spent it all, and then broke, hungry, and friendless, came back home as a last resort. I've got to tell you, that kid really ticks me off. I never read that parable without feeling my blood pressure rise. Just in case you're feeling a bit too calm and relaxed at the moment, let me refresh your memory on the details.

Then Jesus said, "There was once a man who had two sons. The younger said to his father, 'Father, I want right now what's coming to me.'

"So the father divided the property between them. It wasn't long before the younger son packed his bags and left for a distant country. There, undisciplined and dissipated, he wasted everything he had. After he had gone through all his money, there was a bad famine all through that country and he began to hurt. He signed on with a citizen there who assigned him to his fields to slop the pigs. He was so hungry he would have eaten the corncobs in the pig slop, but no one would give him any.

"That brought him to his senses. He said, 'All those farmhands working for my father sit down to three meals a day, and here I am starving to death. I'm going back to my father. I'll say to him, 'Father, I've sinned against God, I've sinned before you; I don't deserve to be called your son. Take me on as a hired hand.' He got right up and went home to his father.

"When he was still a long way off, his father saw him. His heart pounding, he ran out, embraced him, and kissed him. The son started his speech: 'Father, I've sinned against God, I've sinned before you; I don't deserve to be called your son ever again.'

"But the father wasn't listening. He was calling to the servants, 'Quick. Bring a clean set of clothes and dress him. Put the family ring on his finger and sandals on his feet. Then get a grain-fed heifer and roast it. We're going to feast! We're going to have a wonderful time! My son is here—given up for dead and now alive! Given up for lost and now found!' And they began to have a wonderful time" (Luke 15 THE MESSAGE).

Let's sit a minute with the cheeky proposal this kid makes when he tells his dad he wants his money . . . now! That demand was not only hurtful and offensive, it was unheard of in his society. According to the custom of the time, if a father signed over his possessions to his son, the father still had the right to live off the interest as long as he lived. But in this case, the boy demanded not only his inheritance, but also the interest to which he had no right until his father's death. In other words, "Dad, I can't stand around waiting for you to die; let's just pretend you've already croaked."

In addition to the untraditional and disrespectful demand for his inheritance, the son also packed his bags and left "for a distant country." According to Bible commentators, in that time and culture leaving would not have been viewed as a youthful and understandable desire to see the world, but rather as a rejection of the traditions that had been handed down from generation to generation—a serious betrayal of the values of home and country.

Then there's the "undisciplined and dissipated" spending of a very considerable amount of money, which does not seem to bother this boy until the cash is gone. When he's reduced to the most basic human needs of food and shelter, when he's literally starving to death, then he decides to play the role of repentant sinner, go home, and insist he's unworthy to be a son. Maybe he thinks that this manipulative ploy will win over his father and possibly divert his attention from the fact that the kid is coming home penniless, disgraced, and with the unmistakable stench of pig slop clinging to his clothes.

Now am I missing something? As you read the prodigal's account, is there any indication of a softening of this boy's heart, any genuine contrition? Do you sense that he's lamenting, "I've been so foolish, so wrong, so selfish, and so insensitive to my loving father. What I've done to him is unforgivable." I certainly don't see that spirit. In my opinion, the kid has cared only for himself, his needs, and his pleasures from the very beginning. His planned apology was simply a strategy—an effort at what he hoped would be good politics.

Contrary to my hard-boiled, even cynical and suspicious interpretation of the boy's repentance, the father, who has apparently been watching and waiting for his son since he left, stretches out his arms in welcome the second he sees the kid approaching. Dad even runs to meet him. When they rush into each other's arms, the boy begins his prepared speech—"but the father wasn't listening." The father has already forgiven him; the father can think of only one thing, and that is to have a joyous celebration of welcome. I would have required a convincing story of contrition and then . . . maybe . . . macaroni and cheese for dinner.

Of all the parables Jesus told, this is the one that most clearly illustrates the unconditional love and grace of the heavenly Father. We see him portrayed as the father whose arms never cease to be outstretched toward us. We see him as the father who does not require elaborate or heartrending words of confession. The only ticket the wretched child needed to swing open the gates of home was a simple decision to return.

I well up with tears at this example of tender love and I can only say, "That's grace . . . utterly outrageous grace." Obviously, it's not something I extend easily. By contrast, God extends it effortlessly.

Interestingly enough, grace is a word Jesus never used. He did, however, live it, and teach it consistently. The Bible never gives us a tidy, one-sentence definition of the term, but a couple of contemporary authors have made statements

about it that I find particularly succinct. Consider David Sea-
mands' simple definition: "Grace is God's love in action
toward those who do not deserve it."

Or Chuck Swindoll's definitive statement:

> To show grace is to extend favor or kindness to one
> who doesn't deserve it and can never earn it. Receiv-
> ing God's acceptance by grace stands in sharp con-
> trast to earning it on the basis of works. Every time
> the thought of grace appears, there is the idea of its
> being undeserved. In no way is the recipient getting
> what he or she deserves.

That takes us right back to the Prodigal Son parable. We
see grace extended by the father to this selfish, rebellious,
immature, demanding, and utterly self-serving young man.
He didn't earn that grace nor did he deserve it, but grace he
received. Through that parable, Jesus simply wanted to illustrate dramatically and clearly that we are loved by God the
Father—loved beyond measure, loved beyond comprehension, and yes, loved beyond what we deserve. Through
Christ, God purchased for us a ticket to the greatest show on
earth: the unveiling of his outrageous grace and truth in our
own lives. Once we have the ticket in hand, we are boosted
into the thrilling adventure of living as the beloved children
of a heavenly Father.

Some of us have had wonderful earthly fathers who,
though they have loved us imperfectly, have nonetheless
given us a foundation sufficiently secure to be able to believe
and receive the depths of God's father-love. But many more
of us can no more grasp the reality of this kind of love than
dance and cavort with ease on a circus high wire.

Perhaps the only concept you have of a father is one who abused you physically or sexually. Life with him was a living nightmare, and even today, because of him, you not only distrust the concept of the good Father, you reject the concept of even a good man.

Perhaps you were not abused in those ways but were instead ignored, almost erased as a person by a father who was totally indifferent to you. It's as if your existence, your very being, was never even noticed; he simply did not seem to see you or care.

Or maybe you had a father whose criticism of you was so constant, so harsh, so annihilating to your sense of self that you've grown into a person who never feels worthy, never feels good enough. And certainly, you don't feel good enough for a Father like God.

Maybe your father simply left . . . abandoned you totally. And though you may have seen him occasionally, more often than not he wasn't there when you desperately needed him or wanted him. That sense of loss may be excruciating to you.

Into all this human pain and disappointment, God comes to you with an outrageously attractive, hard-to-comprehend offer: he wants to be your Father. He wants to be the Father who never hurts you or is inappropriate with you. He wants to be the Father who knows you're there and notices your every move with tender attention. He wants to be the Father who does not criticize or condemn, who will never leave you or abandon you.

Amazingly enough, he has a plan by which all this can happen, a plan by which you can indeed have him as a Father. Simply put, he wants to adopt you. Ephesians 1:5 says, "He predestined us to be adopted as his [children] through Jesus

Christ." When did he come up with that plan? "He chose us in him before the creation of the world" (Ephesians 1:4). In other words, before the world was even in place, God determined to be your adoptive Father, and to make that adoption possible through Jesus Christ and his death on the cross.

You can't be adopted without Jesus because you fall short of God's standard for perfection; your born-into-sin state separates you from your heavenly Father. But because Jesus died for your imperfection—not just some of it, but all of it—you can become pure, cleansed, and forgiven of that sin when you confess it and then acknowledge Jesus' death as your payment for that sin. First John 1:9 says, "If we confess our sins, he is faithful and just and will forgive us our sins and purify us from all unrighteousness."

Now that's fantastic, but here's where you have to make a decision. This is where the adoption concept figures in. John 1:12–13 says, "To all who received him, to those who believed in his name, he gave the right to become children of God—children born not of natural descent, nor of human decision or a husband's will, but born of God." Who's all this for? Those who believe and receive Jesus as Savior. Those people then become the adopted "children of God."

It's as if Jesus takes our "ticket" of repentance at the gates of heaven, cleans us up, and then takes us to the Father and says, "Here she is, Father, your totally cleansed, completely forgiven, newly adopted daughter." God stretches out his Father arms, scoops us up into his divine embrace, and says, "Welcome home! I've been waiting for you. Let's party!"

That is our outrageous position with the Father who loves us unconditionally and never turns away. What makes that truth even more tender is the use of the word *Abba*, which in the Hebrew means "daddy." We never get too old or too sophisticated to at times long for a daddy, one into whose lap we can crawl and be held, soothed, and comforted. Hosea 14:3 says, "In you the fatherless find compassion." We don't find reprimand, rebuke, or criticism in that Daddy lap; we find compassion for our weakness, compassion for our fatigue, compassion for our many questions, and inexhaustible compassion and forgiveness for our sins.

With your head resting securely against the chest of your heavenly Father, luxuriate in these words from Deuteronomy 33:12:

> Let the beloved of the LORD rest secure in him;
> for he shields him all day long,
> And the one the LORD loves rests between his shoulders.

Because of Jesus, you have a ticket to ride into every day, and ultimately into eternity—home forever in the tender, tenacious embrace of God. ☆

Sideshow

A Prodigal with Promise
by BARBARA JOHNSON

Lloyd Ogilvie, now chaplain of the U.S. Senate, was the commencement speaker at our son Larry's graduation from junior college. Larry was awarded many honors that night, and after the ceremony, Dr. Ogilvie sought us out to congratulate us on having such a fine son. "God has his hand on this boy," he told us. "He's going to use him in a wonderful way."

The very next day, I learned that Larry was a homosexual. That discovery resulted in some ugly scenes between Larry and me, which ultimately led to his estrangement from our family for eleven years. Many times during that long estrangement, Dr. Ogilvie's words of praise and promise replayed themselves in my mind. And each time I shuddered to think how wrong he had been about Larry. *Dr. Ogilvie, if you only knew . . .*

A lot of things changed during the eleven years Larry was gone, and the biggest change occurred in me. God changed my heart of stone into a heart of flesh, and I realized that God still loved Larry, no matter what he'd done—just as he still loved me, no matter what sins I'd committed. Some people think it's outrageous, but the truth is, as someone said, God loves all the flowers, even the wild ones that grow on the side of the road.

After eleven years, Larry called and asked if he could come home. I answered, "Sure, honey. Come on home." God restored our family.

A few years ago when I was a guest on Dr. James Dobson's radio program, "Focus on the Family," Dr. Dobson surprised me by calling Larry and inviting him to comment on what we'd learned from our experience. Larry's words moved me so much that I carry a tape of the broadcast everywhere I go. He closed his comments by saying: "If we as Christians can purpose in our hearts to be kind and loving in all that we do and put away a condemning spirit and learn the fear of the Lord, then surely the light of Christ will be able to shine in our disbelieving world, and restoration and revival will take root in the lives of those that we touch on a daily basis."

Since then I've included Larry's complete message in one of my books and played the tape of his voice to audiences across the country. Wherever I speak I urge parents to show their children unconditional love, to do what Jesus would do and extend love to all God's children, even the wild ones who live outside the mainstream.

By now more than a million people have seen or heard Larry's message asking believers to "put away a condemning spirit." Sometimes I have to chuckle, thinking that Lloyd Ogilvie's prediction came true after all. God has used Larry to touch a lot of people's lives. It probably wasn't the way Dr. Ogilvie had in mind. But God has a wonderful way of using "the least of these" to teach us his truths. ☆

Step Right Up

by LUCI SWINDOLL

I loved Fern the minute we were introduced. When I first met her I could never have imagined the depth of this beautifully exotic woman with whom I was speaking. But by the end of that evening—a picnic in the park with mutual friends, coffee in their home, and sitting in rapt attention while I heard her story—I realized I was in the presence of a remarkable individual.

Born to wealthy parents in the early thirties, Fern spent the first five years of her life in some form of day care with her two sisters, a nurse, and a dog. The dog was her best friend. Her parents visited the nursery an hour a day to see their daughters. Four English children came to live with them during World War II, the eldest of whom (a sixteen-year-old boy) sexually molested her. Fern's parents divorced, and alcohol became her mother's constant companion and crutch. Over a six-year span, Fern's mother moved the girls to five different houses and seven different schools.

Eventually Fern's mother married an abusive man who was loud, vulgar, and physically attracted to Fern. As a result of mothering her own mother and dodging the unwanted advances of her stepfather, she learned to trust no one. Her dogs and horses became her soul mates. She played with them, loved them, talked with them, and told them she would never, ever drink.

At eighteen, Fern married an "older man" of twenty-four, expecting to be taken care of for the rest of her life. The minute the wedding was over, however, her husband set about trying to completely change her. He told her she was too hairy, too heavy, and talked with her hands too much. He decided what she should weigh. If she was even half a pound over his prescribed weight, he criticized her. It wasn't long before she was addicted to diet pills, a bondage that lasted for over forty years.

Three months after her marriage, and one month pregnant, she came home to find another woman in her bed. She was encouraged to join them or get out and wait. She got out!

For three and a half years Fern was married to her first husband, making it through the horror of it all with the help of her animals. This marriage produced a daughter, a son, an abortion, and a lover of her own. Leaving New York, she went to California for a divorce, and then became involved in an affair with a woman. When she returned home she had numerous sexual relationships—with both men and women—as well as opportunities as a popular model, showgirl, and movie actress. "Richard Avedon was the first man who ever told me I was beautiful," she said with a smile.

After her first divorce, she married a man twelve years her senior . . . her "very own alcoholic." Amazingly, they stayed together nine years, and had a son and daughter. But at thirty-seven, with four teenagers in the home, she had a twenty-three-year-old lover coming in and out her bedroom window.

Then Fern met her third husband, Felix DeNar Vaez— the first really positive influence in her life. Because he loved her and she knew it, she tried to clean up her life. She wasn't very successful. For nineteen years they were together, then they married. During this time she was in the movie *Hair*, experimenting with cocaine.

Upon retirement, Felix and Fern moved to Florida, where he took her to church for the first time in her life. She'd found fame and fortune, yet was always seeking so much more. There was an empty void in the pit of her stomach.

During the church service one Sunday as Scripture was being read, Fern heard deep in her heart the words of the Lord, "Come to me." Inexplicably full of emotion and resolve, she responded, "It is me, Lord. I have heard you calling in the night; I will go, Lord, if you will lead me; I will hold your people in my heart." She said, "I was smitten. At the age of sixty-one Jesus had come into my life."

She told her husband she'd fallen in love with another Man. That was the only experience that seemed comparable. Felix replied, "Are you going to tell me his name?"

"Yes. His name is Jesus."

"I'm so happy for you," Felix said. "Do you remember a year ago I told you I had found my serenity? That's the way it came to me."

A few months later, as Felix was watching TV, his heart suddenly stopped and he was gone. Although Fern felt adrift, she knew she wasn't alone. She had her "new Love." She knew she was going to be safe forever. The outrageous thing that had happened to her became her sole reason for living.

As the months progressed, she began to share Christ with her friends, spend more time with the Lord, tell her story to individuals and groups, and put the Lord first in her life. Now she asks him daily, "What do you want from me?"

"God cleaned up my life," Fern explains, "which was so revolting I can't even tell you. I'm just blessed! You know, I've had an awful lot of men in my life—all imperfect—and I didn't want to share them with anyone. And now that I've found the Perfect Man, I want to share him with everybody!"

Now *that* is God's transforming grace. Fern found herself literally invaded by the God of the universe. He loved her and gave her a new heart, a new life, a new passion. It wasn't just a philosophical change she experienced; it was a total metamorphosis. It was outrageous!

Fern's story is more dramatic than most, for sure. But it so beautifully illustrates the power of God in a life. My coauthors have experienced the same transforming grace. God has proven himself the great provider just at their time of greatest need. One has lost a baby and her husband, one suffered clinical depression, one spent years a prisoner in her own home addicted to fear, one was the victim of tremendous racial abuse, one has lost two grown sons and was severely disappointed by the lifestyle of a third. What tragic circumstances in life. Enough heartache to bury a person. And yet, what brought these women of faith together? Joy. A conference on joy. Imagine! God's transforming grace reconstructed the life of Fern who possessed everything, yet had nothing. And that same grace enabled my friends to transcend life's greatest sorrows and emerge with testimonies of joy.

This unmerited favor from God not only secures our eternal salvation, but it also empowers us to keep walking steadily through life's trials and torments. Because we have received "so great a Grace," our lives are altogether different. We have the ability to live on a different plane. Different values and standards for behavior guide us. It's all wrapped up in the word *abundance*. No longer do we merely survive, but we live fully; no longer endure but enjoy; no longer walk a tightrope but relax completely. God's outrageous grace has given us an abundant life.

Because we are given abundance out of God's storehouse of riches, we're able to give abundantly—without holding back or expecting the same treatment. Because we haven't received what we deserve (thankfully!), we can give to others, regardless of what they deserve. The natural response to grace is Fern's comment: "I'm just blessed." Like her, we want to pass on the blessing.

The basis for this kind of giving and responding is characterized in 2 Corinthians 4:15: "All this is for your benefit, so that the grace that is reaching more and more people may cause thanksgiving to overflow to the glory of God." I was privileged to witness this kind of greatheartedness in action in 1997, when three of my dearest friends and I took a cruise from Santiago, Chile, to Buenos Aires, Argentina, around Cape Horn. The adventure included an opportunity to fly over the continent of Antarctica.

On the day we were to make the Antarctic overflight (the highlight of the whole vacation for which we'd paid extra), we were like kids on a field trip. Everyone was assured a window seat on the plane in order to experience the best viewing. We were ready to get our money's worth!

About fifty passengers boarded the bus to be driven from the dock in Punta Arenas to the airfield. There was joking, laughter, picture taking, and swapping of stories. When we got to the plane, there was a long line to get our designated seat assignments, so some of us got on board faster than others. That's when we discovered the dreadful truth: everybody didn't get a window seat. Ohmygosh!

Let me just say, we had a very good opportunity to see humanity in the raw! Tempers flared, voices raised, fists doubled, and the fun and cheer we'd just enjoyed on the bus got obliterated in the jetway. This was not a good sign.

There was finally such commotion and verbal animosity among those who didn't get window seats directed toward those of us who did that the pilot came on the loudspeaker with the suggestion, "If you will just employ a little goodwill and share your window seats, we can take off." Share? Did he say *share?* What an absurd thought! The pilot should be shot!

One man was especially furious, mortified, incensed. He threw dirty looks at everybody—even forcibly grabbed the microphone and announced, "If this plane takes off it'll be over my dead body. I paid for a window seat and we're not leaving here until I get one!" Some passengers shouted back.

Others, like yours truly, simply stared. "Stay above the fray" is my motto!

My friend Ney Bailey, who was in the window seat behind mine, whispered that she'd be glad to offer them her seat, when suddenly, out of the blue, our own Mary Graham stood up across the aisle and with the sweetest smile in the world said, "Here, take mine."

You could have heard a pin drop. Disarmed and befuddled, Big Mouth began to backpedal. "No . . . I don't want yours, I want my own. I paid for my own seat."

Mary wouldn't take no for an answer. "Really, I don't mind. I'm not taking pictures anyway, and I'll go over and sit by Luci. She'll let me lean across her and see. I'll help her change film and she can use me as a camera prop. Come on, take it. I insist." All the while she was gathering her things and moving into my row.

With a bewildered look on his face, this very unhappy man, with his angry wife beside him, took Mary's seat. And (get this), moments after we were airborne they both fell fast asleep and missed that whole array of gorgeous floating icebergs. I don't think they awakened until we got back to Punta Arenas. Meanwhile, on our side of the plane, Mary and I had a wonderful time sharing the joy of seeing that cold, windy, stupendously beautiful region of the earth's surface right out our shared window. We switched back and forth from one seat to the other, sharing the experience with Marilyn and Ney. We didn't miss a thing, and have the pictures to prove it. Mary even brought us all little treats and passed them out like a stewardess. Such fun!

But the story doesn't end there. That evening at our dinner table, a huge, expensive bottle of champagne was delivered to the one and only Mary Graham by her very grateful "new friend." He could not have been more verbally appreciative for the kindness and gratitude he and his wife felt because of Mary's generosity ... completely unmerited. (Frankly, I wanted to leave the guy on the runway and mow him down as we took off.) Mary won this couple's hearts, and I do believe everybody on board heard the story. She became the darling of the cruise line as well as the couple. She had invitations to sit at their table, to visit with them at every opportunity, to come to their home, to be adopted into their family of two.

This act of goodwill from Mary's heart wasn't necessarily easy. The angry couple didn't receive their just desserts. Everybody on the plane (except for Mary, I guess) wanted to handcuff them into aisle seats. But Mary saw it differently, and that's the whole point. She witnessed the unpleasantness, never entered into it, didn't take up their offense, and the Lord, who lives abundantly in her heart, gave her the right spirit and proper words to melt their unkindness. She responded out of the truth in Proverbs 15:1: "A gentle answer turns away wrath, but a harsh word stirs up anger." (Incidentally, Mary is the vice president for the Women of Faith conferences. She works with the speakers so is quite accustomed to taming lions or killing giants. Ahem.)

Everybody experiences difficult situations in life. Everybody. Things that make us want to scream out or give up. Deprivations. Sacrifices. Losses. Misunderstandings. But isn't there some way for the Christian to respond without getting mad at God? Otherwise, what's the good of our faith? There has to be some key to being joyful in the midst of discouraging circumstances and crabby people. What is it?

It's taking God at his Word. It's believing he will do what he says, no matter how things look or how we feel. Nobody said it would be easy. If you find any Scripture that even hints that life will be easy, call me collect. Please. But I can tell you now . . . it ain't in there! However, trusting God with everything we have, everything we are, every problem that is ours, every loss we endure, every battle we face, every person who disappoints us—with thanksgiving—gives us the grace to come through it with flying colors. Colossians 2:6–7 contains the recipe for joyful living: "And now just as you trusted Christ to save you, trust him, too, for each day's problems; live in vital union with him. Let your roots grow down into him and draw up nourishment from him. See that you go on growing in the Lord, and become strong and vigorous in the truth you were taught. Let your lives overflow with joy and thanksgiving for all he has done" (LB).

There's an old hymn that goes,

> *When we walk with the Lord in the light of his word,*
> *What a glory he sheds on our way!*
> *When we do his good will, he abides with us still,*
> *And with all who will trust and obey.*
> *Not a burden we bear, not a sorrow we share,*
> *But our toil he doth richly repay;*
> *Not a grief nor a loss, not a frown nor a cross,*
> *But is blest if we trust and obey.*

I love the line, "but our toil he doth richly repay" because the word *richly* is a word of abundance. Christ doesn't have to repay anything at all, ever—much less from the storehouse of his abundant riches. But he does.

Out of what she refers to as her "revolting" life, God gave my friend Fern abundant love and peace. His blessing. Out of the sorrows of their losses, God gave my Women of Faith cohorts his abundant joy and hope. His blessing. Out of the rotten attitude of disgruntled fellow travelers, God gave my friend Mary the freedom to speak up with words of graciousness. Again, his blessing. Each of these women was "richly repaid" because she stepped right up to ringside and took part in God's incomparable demonstration of grace and mercy. Will you do the same? ☆

Sideshow

Boomerang Grace
by **BARBARA JOHNSON**

One day in the early autumn, an old, retired schoolteacher in a small town called a phone number listed in a classified ad for firewood. An answering machine picked up the call, and a man's gravelly voice instructed her to leave a message. Speaking slowly in her best schoolteacher voice, she carefully gave her full name, address, and phone number, and said she was interested in buying some wood for the winter.

No one returned her call, but the next day when she came home from her volunteer time at the library, the woman found two cords of wood stacked neatly in the yard. A heavy plastic tarp had been tied securely to the end pieces to keep the wood dry. Still in the dark about the woodcutter's identity, she expected to find a bill stuck in the door, but there was none. She checked the mailbox, too, but it was empty. The neighbors had been gone when the anonymous gentleman brought the wood. The schoolteacher called the newspaper office, but the ad-taker said they no longer had a record of the man who'd advertised the wood.

Completely mystified, the woman waited for a bill to come in the mail. Two weeks went by. Then a month. Eventually the woman forgot about the unknown woodcutter.

Meanwhile the firewood cured, and when the temperature dropped unexpectedly on the first day of November, the schoolteacher reached under the plastic tarp and pulled two sticks of firewood from the middle of the stack. As she did, a piece of notepaper fluttered to the ground. Coarse, angular writing filled the page. "Dear Mrs. Martin," the unsigned note said, "thank you for teaching my boy to be smart so he don't have to cut wood for a living."

Standing in front of her fireplace later that evening, the old teacher stared into the crackling flames and smiled. And the fire, filled with a thousand boys' faces, smiled back at her.

Everything we have to give . . .

everything we receive out of God's abundance . . .

is grace. ☆

Part 3

God's
Outrageous
Peace

Remember the Safety Net

by PATSY CLAIRMONT

When I tuned into the news last night, the famous circus act, the Flying Wallendas, was being filmed in Detroit. The group was performing its tightrope act without a net. Five men formed a pyramid by carrying poles on their shoulders. Above their heads on attached poles were two women on bicycles clutching balancing bars. The seven-person troupe inched its way across the wire while spectators (clowns, too) held their breath.

Finally, the Wallendas arrived safely on the other side. Once they descended and were on the sawdust trail, one by one they approached a man sitting on the sidelines, leaned down, and hugged him. He, too, was a Wallenda, but his flying days had come to an abrupt end fourteen years before in Detroit when he'd performed the same stunt, but with a tragic result. The fall left this man wheelchair-bound.

The Wallendas had decided as a troupe that they needed to return to the scene of their tragedy and break the stigma that accident had left on their reputation and in their memories. But more impressive to me than their bravery was the scene that took place before they stepped out to face their fear. The Wallendas formed a circle of prayer. One of the men prayed aloud for the God of peace to guide their steps.

He acknowledged that the Lord was ultimately in control of all things, and then he closed their prayer time with the words, "In Jesus' name, amen."

Amen! Jesus, our ultimate safety net! He is the one who offers us the confidence that no matter how risky life becomes or what tragedy befalls us, he will be our peacemaker. I don't know about you, but understanding that adds to my security. No matter how high I set my trapeze, how devastating my fall, or even how debilitating my crash, he will be there for me. You see, our safety is not in the Lord preventing all our falls, but in the net of peace he spreads beneath regardless of what befalls us. He ultimately will use our slips and spills. Plus, when we fall, he helps us begin again.

This peace-producing information is especially important to clowns because we flub up a lot. (Honk!) I don't know if it's our overstated shoes, the accentuated schnozzola, the humor at all costs, our need for the spotlight, or our self-effacing ways that trip us up, but we sure know how to stumble about, causing our peace to seem more like pieces.

But God's peace isn't fragile. Not only can't it be broken; it is powerful. I remember years ago reading a devotion by Dr. Robert Schuller. He told of two artists who were commissioned to render a picture depicting peace. One painted a tranquil setting with a mirrored lake that reflected lovely draping trees and a glorious mountain backdrop. Wildflowers filled the surrounding fields while butterflies fluttered about. The scene was picture-perfect.

The other artist painted a thunderous waterfall crashing down onto the jagged rocks below, spewing foam and water in all directions. Next to the waterfall he painted a tree that leaned precariously over the water's edge. One of the tree limbs stretched out close to the threatening falls. There, on the slender twigs of the limb within inches of harm's way, was a nest. In the nest was a mother bird, and she was . . . asleep.

I love that outrageous picture. In fact that's a five-star honker! Honk! Honk! Honk! Honk! Honk! Okay, okay, I just had to show my appreciation, and my seltzer bottle didn't seem appropriate. You see, that artist understood that it isn't the absence of problems that demonstrates peace, but being able to rest in the midst of turmoil and threat. That's when we exemplify the "peace that passes understanding."

I've watched safely—yet nervously—from the circus floor as high-wire performers, like birds out on shaky limbs, have teetered precariously. My heart stays in my throat until the aerialist is back on her platform (nest). Even then the ledge she hops on seems so, so . . . petite. If I were to scale the ladder (fat chance), I'd want a platform the size of New Jersey under my ballet slippers. I'd also demand a Velcro high wire as well as Velcro footwear, gloves, helmet, tights, and inflatable tutu. Oh, yes, one other detail—I'd lower the wire to about three feet above the sawdust floor . . . with a safety net below.

That, girlfriends, is the truth about my humanity. But the truth of Christ's divinity is that he offers us peace that does not require all to be picture-perfect. It's a good thing because life is often jagged, filled with thunderous people, leaving us feeling as though we are out on a limb or a very slender high wire. Hmm, perhaps we should build a nest (in the net of his peace) and take a siesta.

Ooh, ooh, an entertaining picture just scampered through my mind. Imagine my five outrageous friends lined up next to me, all of us in inflatable tutus. Honk! Not exactly a peaceful thought, but a funny one.

One thing you won't want to miss are my three-ring circus buddies Marilyn, Thelma, Barbara, and Sheila (minus their tutus—oops, that doesn't sound right. Honk!) as they expand our picture of peace. ☆

Chapter 7

Flying Through the Air with the Greatest of Ease

by SHEILA WALSH

It was my first visit to Las Vegas—city of lights and slot machines and all-you-can-eat buffets. I had a concert at a local church on Saturday night, and I flew in a day early to see the sights. My hosts made a reservation for me at a hotel on the strip called Circus Circus. I checked in, took a quick shower, and headed down to the lobby.

This was no hotel lobby as I understood the term. Row upon row of would-be millionaires sat with buckets of coins, feeding them into ravenous machines which occasionally coughed back a few quarters. I wondered for a moment if God would bless me at the card tables if I tithed the results—but then I determined to catch hold of myself before the spirit of Vegas took over.

I walked toward a crowd that was gathering at the other end of the lobby and saw that some kind of act was about to begin. "What's happening?" I asked the lady standing beside me, her bucket of coins in one hand and a large, scary look-ing drink in the other.

"It's a trapeze act," she replied. "They're a family. One of the brothers does a triple back somersault."

I stared at her in disbelief. "In the hotel lobby?" I asked, wondering if her drink had drowned her brain cells. But then the lights went out and a spotlight picked up two men and two women in glittering costumes beginning a climb up a rope ladder to a wire suspended over our heads. We watched in awe as the trapeze artists flew above us with the grace of the summer swallows returning to Capistrano. The lights danced across the sequined costumes, and we clapped with relief at each successful trip. Then we communally held our breath as the show built to a climax for the famous triple back somersault. It was flawless, magnificent, spectacular.

When the show was over the performers descended the rope ladder and donned satin capes. Then, to my amazement, they headed straight toward me. I panicked. Were they looking for an audience volunteer? I tried to formulate a good excuse in my mind ... "I have a bad leg. I'm a member of a small Scot-tish non-ladder climbing denomination." All I knew was I had no desire to end my life in the lobby of this surreal hotel.

When they reached me, one of the girls threw her arms round me and said, "Praise God, Sheila! We're coming to your concert tomorrow night." You could have bowled me over with a sequined feather! It turned out that they were a Christian family and members of the church I'd be singing at. How bizarre! But what a relief!

I took this opportunity to ask some very basic questions: "Are you afraid? Have you ever fallen? Has that costume ever split up there? Can you dry-clean sequins?"

Mr. Triple Somersault told me, "This is our life, we trust each other, we're family, we work on this."

It's pretty outrageous to fly through the lobby of a hotel for a living, but what is more outrageous is that this is exactly what we're called to do as we fly out in faith, trusting Christ, supported by outrageous peace. The trapeze family was very good, but they were human. They could drop one another. Someone could fall.

Do you ever wonder about your own safety when you're flying out in faith? Do you feel like you're swinging out there on your own with no net? Not a chance! How do I know? Well, first of all it's written in indelible ink in God's Word—his unchanging, infallible, not-a-chance-it's-going-to-happen Word. Remember?

"Be strong and courageous. Do not be afraid or terrified because of them, for the LORD your God goes with you; he will never leave you nor forsake you" (Deuteronomy 31:6).

"I lift up my eyes to the hills—where does my help come from? My help comes from the LORD, the Maker of heaven and earth. He will not let your foot slip—he who watches over you will not slumber" (Psalm 121:1–3).

"Peace I leave with you; my peace I give you. I do not give to you as the world gives. Do not let your hearts be troubled and do not be afraid" (John 14:27).

God's Word is bursting at the seams with promises as awesome as these. And then we have our own stories to remind us of God's peace-producing faithfulness. On my journey toward learning to trust God, one of the firmest stones to stand on is my memory of past experience: When I look back down the path and see how he has led me, I see that doors he closed that I wanted opened would have been the wrong doors to have gone through. For me, relaxing in God's peace means letting go of that "c" word: CONTROL. Scripture tells us to be anxious about nothing, to leave our lives in his hands. But that's been tough for me.

I have recently rerecorded a song called "Trapeze." I wrote it with a couple of friends over ten years ago, but I don't think I understood the lyrics at all until the past couple of years. When I wrote it I was living in London and working at the British Broadcasting Center, hosting the first ever Christian music show on secular television. We were on prime time once a week. It was very exciting to have this opportunity. *TV Guide* devoted a whole page to the show, and there was a sense that God was doing something new in Britain. The show's success opened the door to booking a nationwide tour, which sold out every major music venue in Scotland and England.

The week before the tour was to begin, I lost my voice and everything was canceled. In my disappointment and confusion I wrote,

> *I was the only one*
> *Star of the show*
> *Thought I could make it on my own*
> *Then came the big surprise out of the blue*
> *What is a clown supposed to do*

> *When suddenly I'm falling out of the sky*
> *Don't let me go or I will die*
> *Whose hands are these on my trapeze*
> *Take hold of me or there will be a tragedy.*
> *Whose hands are these on my trapeze*
> *I'm falling free, you rescued me so willingly*
> *On my trapeze.*

Almost ten years later I found myself in a psychiatric hospital, and the words of my own song came back to comfort me. I certainly felt as if I was falling out of the sky, falling fast and hard with no safety net. But what I experienced was the truth of the words I'd written a decade before. When I'd written them, I hoped they were true; now I discovered they were. This was an outrageous discovery for me. Christ not only promises that a net will be there when I'm dangling from the trapeze of life; he *is* the net. What peace. What outrageous peace!

I'm also learning that even though I would never have chosen some parts of the path that God has led me on, now I wouldn't change a single day. I hear that same sentiment from so many women every weekend at Women of Faith conferences. One after another, women share with me parts of their stories—from the devastating to the sublime—and affirm that through it all they have become different women. Whole, godly, rich women. I understand that now. You can study the theory of soaring on the trapeze for years, but until you let go and fly, it's all in your head. You can hope you'll be safe; you can believe that your partner will be there to catch you. But until you let go, it's all just theory and wishful thinking.

I've discovered that when I finally throw myself out there in total abandonment to God, I'm never the same again. For me, learning to trust myself totally into the hands of God had helped me to trust others also. The women I travel and speak with most weekends have become the dearest, most trusted friends of my life. We fly as a team. We're there to catch each other when we fly out in faith. Some weekends I don't fly as well as others, but someone on the team makes up the shortfall and covers the distance. I'm learning that I'm never alone as a child of God.

Think of your own life. Stop for a moment and reflect on any situation where it seemed as if you were on your own, that it was hopeless, that you were forgotten. Remember how you could never have anticipated God showing up, but he did, with flying colors—even if it seemed like he left you dangling just a little too long for comfort!

I remember reading a wonderful letter included in a book called *The Wonders of Prayer*, written in England in 1885 by Major Daniel Webster Whittle. The letter is written by an anonymous sea captain who is relating the events of a voyage in 1876. The captain tells of the unusual shifting currents that held his ship at sea in the same position for five or six days. He prayed repeatedly, "Lord, why are we so hindered and kept in this position?" When his crew finally got the ship to port, they heard of the devastation that had occurred at sea all around them. A ferocious gale had destroyed many vessels, but theirs had been held as if in a quiet circle. If they had been able to move even fifty miles, they would have ended up at the bottom of the ocean. The captain closed his letter with thanks to God, quoting from Deuteronomy 33:12 (KJV), "The beloved of the LORD shall dwell in safety by him, and the LORD shall cover him all the day long." Amen, Captain!

Peace is something that makes no sense to the uninitiated because it is often peace in the midst of circumstances that cry out: turmoil! I think of the disciples as they huddled together in that small room after Jesus had been executed. They were terrified. Nothing made sense to them anymore. They had expected the best and tasted the worst. Peter— loud, salt of the earth, brash, strong, his mouth still sour from his denials that he'd ever met Jesus—was sick to his stomach, sick at heart. And the others were no better: sad, disillusioned, a traveling band with no map, compass, or direction.

And then . . . into their silent hell he came walking. Jesus was alive! They still didn't understand anything very well, but Jesus was alive so everything was different. Do you remember what he said to them? "On the evening of that first day of the week, when the disciples were together, with the doors locked for fear of the Jews, Jesus came and stood among them and said, 'Peace be with you!'" (John 20:19). That changed everything for them. They had been falling out of the sky when suddenly Jesus was under them, above them, all around them. That's his promise to us, too.

I don't know what the circumstances of your life are right now, or how fast you feel you're falling, or whether you're frozen on the bar, afraid to let go and grab hold of God's hands. What I can tell you as a novice flyer is that he is here, right now, and he won't let you go. He will catch you in midair. The net of his faithful love will cushion you when you free-fall.

Whose hands are these on my trapeze
I'm falling free, you rescued me so willingly
On my trapeze.

What peace. What outrageous peace! ☆

Peace on the High Wire
by BARBARA JOHNSON

Last year when the Women of Faith conference was in Buffalo, New York, Bill and I took a few hours off to visit nearby Niagara Falls. What an extraordinary place of beauty and power God created there! Just a short distance above the falls the wide Niagara River seems so peaceful and smooth, and then suddenly it plunges over the edge and thunders into a roaring current of foam and vapor—a natural wonder that is anything but peaceful!

As if the falls themselves weren't spectacular enough, for more than a century daredevils have been performing all sorts of incredible feats there, trying to win recognition for their courage—if not for their amazing lack of common sense! The most famous of these daredevils was a French tightrope walker known as Blondin, who first crossed the Niagara gorge on a tightrope in 1848.

Blondin didn't just walk across the tightrope strung high over the gorge, however. He pushed a wheelbarrow across it too. Another time he carried his manager across on his back. Finally, he carried a pack out to the middle of the high wire. There, hundreds of feet above the churning water, he took out a little wood-burning stove, lit a fire, cooked an omelet, and then lowered it on a china plate to the crew of a boat waiting below!

When I heard that story, the image of a man nonchalantly cooking breakfast on a tightrope strung across a gorge created in my mind a vivid illustration of the Christian walk. As believers, we too are tightrope artists, walking Christ's narrow way that stretches straight and true above life's churning waters. We know it's not an easy rope to walk, and we know there are other ways to cross the river. But we choose this one, carefully placing one foot in front of the other and easing out over the abyss.

Occasionally we wobble, but we do not fall. Balanced on the tightrope, high above the chaos, we experience an outrageous peace. And this peace is ours simply because of what we take across the high wire. Not a balance bar. Not a wheelbarrow. Not a stove for cooking breakfast. Instead, we take the nail-scarred hand of Jesus and step out confidently over the water, knowing that "the LORD will give strength unto his people; the LORD will bless his people with peace" (Psalm 29:11 KJV). ☆

Chapter 8

God in the Odd

by MARILYN MEBERG

When I was a child I wanted desperately to be a preacher. I don't know if that burning desire was nothing more than an effort to walk in my pastor-father's shoes or to defy the gender tradition that women (in those days) didn't become preachers. But at the age of ten it was my practice to gather up as many neighborhood kids as I could to participate in my preaching services.

We had several cords of wood piled by the side of the garage which served as sanctuary seating. I would look up into the indifferent faces of my little parishioners and preach my heart out. Ed Meister would serve as a roving counselor (not easy when you're balancing on a wood pile), encouraging those under conviction to consider the claims of Christ while I softly hummed "Just As I Am."

Generally the only one left in the service by that time was Billy Dipthorne. He played the role of repentant sinner. Sometimes he would sob, cry, and beg forgiveness, but other times he'd insist I was preaching "hooey" and that he didn't believe a word I'd said. It was then that Ed Meister's counseling skills were put to the test, because if Billy Dipthorne huffed off still in his unregenerate state, no one got a fudgesicle at the end of the service. Billy seemed to enjoy that power, which antagonized Ed to the point of occasional violence if Billy refused to become a convert. The conclusions of our services were rarely peaceful.

Sometimes my parents would peek out the kitchen window during one of those meetings to marvel at my evangelistic fervor. Since my father never ranted and raved or even flung his arms about, I'm sure they found my style a bit mystifying. I wonder if either of my parents ever worried about my slightly off-kilter practices. If they did, they never let on. Actually, my father was a bit off-kilter as well; my mother seemed to find us both amusing. Since she was warmly responsive to both of us, I never felt any need to be alarmed by my appreciation of the offbeat or unusual.

Not surprisingly, one of my favorite characteristics of God is what I say in all reverence is his out-of-the-norm, off-the-beaten-path, utterly unique style of doing things. One of my delights in Scripture is finding "God in the odd." It pleases me not only because of my appreciation for the unique, but because there are wonderful lessons to be learned by studying this dimension of God.

Consider Moses who, as an infant, is popped into a little woven basket and placed in the Nile by his loving and concerned mother. This was in an effort to preserve his life from the death sentence pronounced upon all Hebrew babies. He's rescued by the daughter of the very king who instituted the death sentence and subsequently raised as a prince in the palace of the enemy. That's incredible drama, but doesn't that little boat idea strike you as odd? Who but God would even think of it?

Do you remember in Numbers 22, when God spoke to Balaam through the mouth of Balaam's donkey? Balaam had been instructed by God to give a specific message to the king of the Moabites. Balaam took a little license with what he knew to be God's message, so God opened the donkey's mouth, and a two-way conversation began between Balaam and his mule. As a result, Balaam realized God was displeased with him. Confessing his disobedience, Balaam promised to say the very words God had spoken. The donkey shut up when Balaam shaped up. Don't tell me that's not odd.

One of my all-time favorite God-in-the-odd narratives is when God led Ezekiel out into the middle of a valley full of dry bones. God walked Ezekiel back and forth among the bones and then commanded, "Prophesy to these bones" (Ezekiel 37:4). Can you not imagine a bit of whiplash from Ezekiel? How in the world does one start a conversation with a pile of bones? Ezekiel didn't have to ponder that very long because God told the prophet exactly what to say. "So I prophesied as I was commanded. And as I was prophesying, there was a noise, a rattling sound, and the bones came together, bone to bone" (Ezekiel 37:7–8). Mind boggling!

And then there's the familiar story of David and Goliath: scrawny boy with slingshot knocks out a Godzilla of a man with a single well-placed rock to the forehead. Now isn't that the kind of stuff kids read in comic books? But this story is in the Word of God!

Why do you suppose God seems to revel in these unusual, creative, and peculiar methods of doing things? For one thing, God wants us to remember that we're not like him. We don't do things the same way; we don't even think in the same way (Isaiah 55:8). I never in a million years would have thought to have Jesus born in a barn. Mercy! The Son of God . . . the Savior of the world . . . the Creator and Ruler of all the galaxies in all the universes, nestled in dirty hay in a smelly barn. How utterly unthinkable!

And doesn't it kind of blow your mind that Jesus chose the men he did to be his companions and disciples? I would have screened them for verbal skills, the ability to interact with a cross section of society, and certainly grooming would have been a major consideration. But no . . . Jesus chose uneducated, rough-hewn, common laborers to not only participate in his brief earthly ministry but to then, after the Ascension, establish the church and spread the Good News of who Jesus is: the long-awaited Messiah, the One sent from God to free all of humankind from darkness and death. Colossal news out of the mouths of ordinary guys, handpicked by God the Son. Amazing!

I can't begin to answer the question of why God does what he does in ways that I consider a bit off-kilter and odd, but I can certainly describe the lessons I learn from these methods. These lessons contribute a tremendous peace and soul satisfaction when fully understood. My peace is bolstered when I contemplate as well as experience God's totally unfathomable workings in my life. That's because I know for a fact that he's around! There's no other explanation for how things are going . . . or not going. Sometimes his odd workings get my attention to the point of whiplashing me into a neck brace! My response is always "who but God?" When I have a "who but God" reaction, I know who to credit for whatever is going on in my life—and that assurance produces peace.

Not only do these peculiar methods get my attention and cause me to focus on him rather than on myself, but I am also reminded that God does what he does to underscore who he is. Let's flip back to that incredible story in Ezekiel 37. When God told Ezekiel to chat with the bones, the purpose was hugely significant as a prophecy to the Israelite people. In this unforgettable image of bones coming together and life being breathed back into them, God promised his children that he, the giver of all life, the preserver of his chosen people, would reestablish them as a nation:

> Son of man, these bones are the whole house of Israel. They say, "Our bones are dried up and our hope is gone; we are cut off." Therefore prophesy and say to them: "This is what the Sovereign LORD says: O my people, I am going to open your graves and bring you up from them; I will bring you back to the land of Israel." (Ezekiel 37:11–12)

God adds to this unforgettable image, "Then you, my people, will know that I am the LORD!" (v. 13). He underscores that crucial truth by restating it: "Then you will know that I the LORD have spoken and I have done it!" (v. 14).

This passage in Ezekiel suggests a pattern God seems to use as he introduces us to his extraordinary ways. First he gets our attention; then he tells us his purpose: "that you will know that I am the LORD."

We see that pattern in the story of David and Goliath when David says to the scowling, insulted giant: "I come against you in the name of the LORD Almighty, the God of the armies of Israel, whom you have defied. . . . All those gathered here will know that it is not by sword or spear that the LORD saves; for the battle is the LORD's, and he will give all of you into our hands" (1 Samuel 17:45, 47). God does it . . . I don't! What a great peace producer!

I am humbled as well as amazed that God does his extraordinary work through common, ordinary people. Our society puts an inordinate emphasis upon external success and being number one. We even rate people and events according to some numerical hierarchy of acceptability: We have the ten best-dressed list, the ten worst-dressed list, the top-ten box office hits, the *New York Times* best-seller list, to name a few.

I'm not necessarily opposed to these worldly designations, it's just that it doesn't seem to matter a whit to God. Jesus used ordinary flowers, trees, and birds to teach profound lessons about himself and about life. He placed ordinary mud from the ground on the eyes of a blind man and restored his sight. Jesus changed ordinary water into extraordinary wine. He took a lunch of ordinary fish and bread and from them made an extraordinary lunch for five thousand hungry people.

Paul summarizes God's use of the ordinary (and the odd) in a letter to the Corinthians:

> Notice among yourselves, dear brothers, that few of
> you who follow Christ have big names or power or

wealth. Instead, God has deliberately chosen to use ideas the world considers foolish and of little worth in order to shame those people considered by the world as wise and great. He has chosen a plan despised by the world, counted as nothing at all, and used it to bring down to nothing those the world considers great, so that no one anywhere can ever brag in the presence of God. (1 Corinthians 1:26–29 LB)

Once again we see the pattern: God does the unusual so that we recognize his unmistakable hand. Why? "So that no one anywhere can ever brag in the presence of God." I cannot take the credit for how things work out in my life. I cannot brag about my fine insights, good judgment, or special ability. God makes sure that his accomplishments are performed by him; it is his insight, his good judgment, and his ability that brings extraordinary results out of ordinary circumstances.

The irreversible truth of all this imprinted itself upon my mind and spirit a number of years ago. I was moving my parents from Sun City, Arizona, to a retirement home in San Diego. I was anxious about the trip because my parents were in poor health and we had to drive through a portion of desert that was extremely desolate and exceedingly hot. Prior to leaving for the trip, Ken conscientiously had the car serviced, with special attention given to the hoses which might overreact to hot weather. We even prayed over the car together and committed its efficiency and well-being to the Lord. Since Ken was not able to go with me, a friend and I took off for Phoenix, gathered up my parents, and headed out for the day's trip to San Diego.

After lunch in Yuma, we drove off again through the desert. I glanced at my mother who was dozing and looking comfortable; I checked the rearview mirror and noted my father also dozing. I was suffused with gratitude for my big car and its wonderful air-conditioning system as well as for the seemingly effortless way the trip was progressing.

In the midst of this private little praise service, I was amused by a sign pointing to Ocotillo: "Last stop for gas and food." I glanced derisively at what appeared to be an utterly desolate wide spot off the freeway. Grateful that Ocotillo was not included on my Trip-tic, I confidently settled into the cushiony comfort of my car. Only seconds later, I was rousted by a sudden strange hissing sound accompanied with billows of steam curling from beneath the hood. I wheeled into Ocotillo. I had lost power steering, windows, brakes, and of course, air-conditioning.

As we slowly rolled to a stop on what looked to me to be no more than a gravel landing strip for small planes, I felt panic. We opened the car doors to 116-degree heat. I bolted down the strip to what looked to be a garage. It was closed . . . not a sign of life. I dashed back to the little "Food" building with its screen door hanging crookedly by one rusty hinge; it was swinging and banging languidly open and shut, propelled by a searing breeze. I stepped inside—again, not a sign of life. There was a partially full coffee cup on the counter. I stuck my finger in it . . . cold. Whoever drank it was dead; whoever served it was also dead.

I thought, "God, how could you let this happen? My car is dead like everything else in Ocotillo, and in this heat we'll soon be dead too. Ken and I prayed over this car. Doesn't that mean anything? You could maybe let this happen to me, but not to my elderly, unwell parents! After all, they have served you in public ministry for over fifty years. I can't help telling you, God, this is a pretty rotten way to treat them!"

I was sharing some other mutterings with God when I noticed that about two hundred yards behind my still-hissing car was what looked like a tow truck parked beside a sedan. Grabbing my friend, I sprinted toward the truck and car. It was indeed a tow truck. Its driver was staring straight ahead, wordlessly, mechanically raising and lowering a Coke can from his lips to his lap. He seemed oblivious to my heavy breathing.

I glanced at the sedan next to the truck. The stringy-haired driver was drinking his Coke in exactly the same wordless and mechanical manner as the truck driver. His car was filled with filthy looking junk: newspapers, bottles, cans, and miscellaneous tools. Utterly repelled by the car and its occupant, I turned my attention to the truck driver who, after much prodding from me, said he was on his way to San Diego. I explained that my elderly parents, my friend, and I were desperately in need of transportation, and begged him to consider towing my disabled car to our destination. After several labored drags from his Coke can he finally said he would give me a tow but that two of us would "have ta ride with Manuel." Quickly surveying once again that disreputable car and its equally disreputable driver, I groaned inwardly and agreed.

Since I assumed God had let me down, while running back to my car I hatched a totally Godless plan which reflected my determination to take things into my own hands. I figured these two men were probably hatching their own plan, which was to kill us all, take our stuff, and proceed in their mechanical fashion to San Diego. Having now lost my faith as well as my sanctification, I told my friend to put Dad in the tow truck next to the door. She was to sit in the middle and if Tony the truck driver made a move to leave the freeway (which would indicate he planned to kill them), she was to quickly shove Tony out the door, move behind the wheel, and speed off with my father and the car to San Diego.

I had noticed a number of wrenches in Manuel's car, so my plan was to place my mother in the front seat while I sat in back with a wrench held tightly in my fist. If Manuel made a move to pull off the road or harm my mother, I'd belt him over the head, shove him out of the car, and drive us to safety. Somehow, we'd meet up in San Diego.

With that totally unspiritual plan agreed upon between my friend and I (I never revealed it to my parents), I helped my mother into Manuel's filthy car. (I was surprised at how carefully he scraped a spot clear for her to sit. It seemed unnecessary since I knew he planned to kill us fairly soon.)

I crawled into the backseat, picked out a large wrench, and sat poised tensely with my weapon clutched behind my back. We had been on the freeway less than five minutes when Manuel did exactly what I feared he'd do. He pulled off onto a little gravel road that led away from the freeway. My entire body was ready to spring into action and deliver the head blow when he turned woodenly to me and asked without a trace of inflection, "Do you remember where Tony said he was going to stop for gas?" As the car came to a stop, I said with the same flat tone, "No, I don't remember where Tony said we would stop for gas." Manuel then turned the car toward the freeway and, staring straight ahead, said, "We'll wait here." Very soon Tony passed us with my car hoisted up on its little hind legs with everyone in the truck staring straight ahead. As we pulled in behind them on the freeway, I relaxed my grip on the wrench.

After Tony had gassed up his truck we again took off. Within minutes Manuel turned to my mother and, with the same fixed expression and deadpan tone, asked if she minded if he smoked. Ever the gracious lady, Mother told him of course she did not mind. I minded! But he hadn't asked me. He cracked the little window on his side and carefully held the cigarette out of the crack, skillfully exhaling so that no smoke entered the car. I put the wrench down on the floor. Leaning back against the weathered vinyl seat I thought, *Lord, who are these two awful-looking, strange-acting men? Are they angels or something? Bad-looking angels ... certainly not my taste ... but I wonder ...*

Tony knew where the retirement village was so he took us to a garage located just two blocks from our destination. I asked Tony how much I owed him for the hundred-mile tow. Finding myself still reluctant to ascribe good intentions to him, I figured he'd probably charge me a thousand dollars, especially since he'd decided against killing us. With the same expressionless face and voice, he said it would be one hundred dollars.

I couldn't believe it. "Tony," I said, "that's only a dollar a mile ... surely I owe you more than that!"

"No ... no ... that's okay ... I was coming here anyway."

I thanked him profusely and paid him, then I headed back to Manuel who continued to sit in his car staring straight ahead. I thanked him as well and tried to hand him some money. He refused it saying, "No, no ... that's okay ... I was coming here anyway." With tears in my eyes, I dropped the money on the seat beside him and walked away.

Once again, I couldn't mistake God's fingerprints all over my life. My car broke down in one of the hottest, seemingly God-forsaken spots on the face of the earth. To be rescued from that spot I needed two things: a tow truck and a passenger car . . . and there they were by the side of the road, just waiting for me! Those vehicles were driven by two very ordinary, extremely peculiar, God-chosen guys to remind me yet again "that no one anywhere can ever brag in the presence of God" and that his ways are not my ways.

I have pondered that desert experience many times. What was God doing and why? I know he was not dismissing the importance of car maintenance or even our sincere praying over that car prior to making the trip. But every now and then, I need to be reminded of who takes care of me and who is in charge of all the events in my life. When I'm skipping blithely across the high wire, congratulating myself on my confidence and skill, it's easy to forget who my safety net is. Fortunately, God doesn't let me be the star of the show from start to finish. Sometimes he turns things completely upside down so that what is happening does not make sense to me at all! In fact, I lose my balance completely, and I'm forced to cling to him and rest in his peace that passes understanding.

You may find yourself in the middle of circumstances that don't make sense to you. You may be surrounded by people who would never be your choice. Possibly God is reminding you that "the battle is the Lord's" and the way he wins battles is often through people and events we'd never even think of, much less choose. Why does God do this? "So that no one anywhere can ever brag in the presence of God."

Oddly enough, that knowledge takes the pressure off of me. I can quit striving, plotting, maneuvering, and pirouetting on the high wire of life. I am not the star of the show; God is. That brings me outrageous peace. ☆

Sideshow

Heaven's Misfits
by BARBARA JOHNSON

I dreamed I went to heaven,
And I was quite surprised
To see just who had made it to
That home up in the sky:
The ragged, dirty drifter,
The kid who rarely spoke,
The loudmouthed woman down the street—
Was this some kind of joke?
Then I noticed they were staring
Right at me. They made it clear
That all of them were thinking,
"What are *you* doing here?"

Ann Luna

Chapter 9

Shot Out of a Cannon and Lived to Tell About It

by THELMA WELLS

We don't see a lot of cannons around anymore—except in circus acts and cartoons that depict people being shot out of them and laughing all the way. Whoever came up with that idea anyway? I mean, a cannon was a deadly weapon of war. Big, heavy, wrought iron, with an imposing barrel, breech, and firing mechanism that propelled seven-hundred-pound balls that demolished anything or anybody within range.

Sometimes life's heartaches and disappointments look like cannonballs—heading straight toward us. And baby, it ain't funny when you're shot out of the cannon in real life, either. Every week I talk with people who are battling the heavy artillery of life. Depression, oppression, loneliness, barrenness. In fact, I have recorded over forty "Woes of Hurting Women" that people have told me about, ranging from abuse, abandonment, abortion, addiction, adoption— throughout the alphabet to oppression from religious zealots. Seven hundred pounds is a light load for some of these women because they already feel like the weight of the world is on their shoulders.

Sometimes the enemy's ammunition hits us from behind, when we're least expecting it. But more often, I've found, we sit right in the line of fire—voluntarily!

I remember listening to an attorney speak in Daytona Beach, Florida, several years ago. Her sister had been married to a man who was so abusive that all the immediate family members tried to intervene and persuade this young lady to get out of the relationship and get some help. Every time her relatives would succeed in getting her away from her husband, for some reason she would go back to that violent man. She had given her life to Christ at an early age, but apparently she'd never found the inner peace that would have enabled her to move out of the line of fire. Eventually, one of those seven-hundred-pound balls killed her.

What was the problem? Why did this young woman feel literally catapulted into a situation that emotionally and physically destroyed her? In a word: fear! She was afraid to move out of firing range because she didn't believe she could do better. She was so paralyzed by her fears that she allowed herself to die from the abuse she so desperately dreaded.

Through the years, I've discovered four unconscious fears that I believe all of us face every day: the fear of success, the fear of failure, the fear of rejection, and the fear of risk or loss. Whether we admit it or not, whether we're Christian or not, all of us battle with fear. Some of us are positively motivated by our fears; they propel us to take useful, God-inspired action, or to hide under the shadow of his wing until the danger passes by. Others of us are negatively motivated by fear; we allow it to control us to such a degree that we become frozen in the war zone.

When I heard the sad story about the Florida woman who died from abuse, I could relate to some of her experience. When I was a little girl, one of my family members saw fit to lock me in a dark, dingy, stinky, mildewy closet all day every day, without food or water. Abusive? Certainly. And yet I can't say I identify with the abused woman's fear and turmoil. Why? Because, like her, I am a Christian, and have been since I was four years old. My great-grandmother, Granny Sarah Harrell, introduced me to church and a relationship with Jesus, and I grew up being in church seven days a week: Monday for missions; Tuesday for ladies' auxiliary; Wednesday for prayer meeting; Thursday for choir rehearsal; Friday for teachers' meeting; Saturday to help clean up the church; Sunday all day 'cause black folks stayed in church all day on Sunday. I learned the hymns of the faith and heard all the testimonies of the members of the church. I was in Sunday school, Baptist Training Union, and all the children's activities available. I memorized religious poems and Scripture. All I knew was church. Consequently, when I was put into that dungeon of a closet by myself, I would sing hymns until I'd sing myself to sleep.

Little did I understand then that the music I was singing was engulfing me in the protection of the Holy Spirit, who had come to live in me at the moment I accepted Christ. Because my mind was on the songs and not on the problem, I came out of that closet day after day without any—I mean *any*—animosity, bitterness, or despair. The cannon was shooting, but I had a shield: the Spirit of God. The ammunition of abuse was never able to penetrate my soul. In the midst of the battle, I experienced a "peace that passes understanding."

That same peace is available to all those who trust God. So why don't we always experience it? Why do we sometimes sit out in the middle of the battlefield, unprotected, waiting for cannonballs to land on our heads?

There are things we can do to divert the cannonballs while life's battle is raging. There is a barricade we can put up that will insure our safety and surround us with an incomprehensible peace.

I was reminded of these glorious truths while sitting in my hotel room one day preparing for a Women of Faith conference. Thank God for the Holy Bible! As I was reading his Word, I ran across a truth that can give any one of us courage and peace as we wait for the cannons of life to stop blasting.

In his first letter to the Corinthians, the apostle Paul reminds the early believers that they have abundant grace and peace from God the Father and the Lord Jesus Christ. "In him you have been enriched in every way," Paul says. "Therefore you do not lack any spiritual gift as you eagerly wait for our Lord Jesus Christ to be revealed. He will keep you strong to the end, so that you will be blameless on the day of our Lord Jesus Christ. God, who has called you into fellowship with his Son Jesus Christ our Lord, is faithful" (1 Corinthians 1:5, 7–9).

Each one of us is given everything spiritually that we need to remain "strong to the end." In the spiritual realm—the one beyond our physical sight, where God is busy initiating and completing divine activity—all is well. Even when there is chaos in our lives, we can experience indescribable peace because we know that whatever we are going through, God already knows about it and has equipped us to handle it with his grace. It is his faithfulness that gives us confidence and peace.

I can remember a period in my life when I was flat broke. Sometimes I would have only a quarter in my purse. I kept that so if the car broke down or I needed to call someone on the phone, I could. At times I would have a pity party about my financial dilemma. But the party wouldn't last too long because I would begin to think about how blessed I was. I had two good arms, legs, eyes, ears, feet; I could think, work, give, love. When I'd begin thinking about how good God was to me and my family even in that desperate financial state, I would inevitably start praising him for what I had rather than lamenting over what I did not have.

One day while I was driving and listening to gospel music, I found myself thanking God that I had gas in my car. I began to cry tears of joy and actually thank God for that quarter I had in my purse. I affirmed the biblical principle that he would take that twenty-five cents and multiply it. Even though I had no tangible evidence, I was excited about what God was doing for me. I had faith to believe that he would not leave me poor—that in the supernatural realm he had already worked out his divine solutions to my problems.

Nothing spectacular happened that day or in the next few days, but my faith did not waiver. Through prayer and thanksgiving I gained peace that I could not explain. How outrageous is that!

Psalm 62:1–2 says, "My soul finds rest in God alone; my salvation comes from him. He alone is my rock and my salvation; he is my fortress, I will never be shaken." When we realize that our only hope is in Christ Jesus and that trusting in him to help us is the answer to our problems, we put up a protective shield—a fortress—against the cannonballs that hurtle toward us.

When we accept Jesus Christ as our Savior, the Comforter (the Holy Spirit) comes to fill us and to dwell in us. His attributes are peace, love, joy, long-suffering, patience, gentleness, goodness, meekness, faithfulness, and self-control. All nine of those attitudes live in us because he lives in us, but sometimes they lie dormant. I've learned that we need to ask God to manifest all those attributes when warfare is raging in our lives. They are powerful weapons when the tough times come.

One powerful way we can welcome the Holy Spirit's fullness in our spirit is by praising God through song. Besides singing the hymns I learned years ago in church, I sometimes make up songs to sing to God. Nobody hears them but me and God, so it doesn't make any difference if they are lyrical or lovely; they are simply songs from my heart. When I sing, or listen to others sing praise songs on tape, I watch my downtrodden spirit rise and my peace grow.

Life is full of choices every minute of the day. I choose to never have a bad day. I cannot prevent the perplexities of life, but I can choose how I respond to them. Even though I don't let myself have a completely bad day, I certainly have bad moments many days. But I've discovered a foolproof method for moving through them as quickly as possible. When I need a pity party, I literally set my clock for fifteen minutes. Within that time frame, I whine and wail, beat myself up, throw a temper tantrum, break something, or whatever I feel is appropriate to my circumstances at the moment. When the alarm sounds, I know that's my cue to cut it out.

Admittedly, sometimes I've had to set the clock four times before I got it all out of my system! But I think that one hour is long enough to stay in a state of insanity. (That's what it is, you know; letting ourselves be controlled by fear is crazy when Jesus tells us we need not be afraid.) So after I've used up my four times to reset the clock, I force myself to STOP. I force myself to start the praise music. I force myself to pray. Sometimes when I can't think of what to say in prayer, I just say, "Jesus, Jesus, Jesus." The enemy of our soul flees at the name of Jesus. I remind myself that God has not given me a spirit of fear, but of love, power, and a sound mind (2 Timothy 1:7 KJV).

While in this process of trying to regain my sound mind, I feel that peace I can't describe bubbling up inside me. I calm down, I start thinking more clearly. I'm not as inclined to make irrational decisions.

If this works for me, it will certainly work for you. God doesn't love me any more than he loves you. If you doubt it, just look at your life. Not only have you been in the way of some seven-hundred-pound cannonballs, you've been shot out of that cannon more than once and you lived to tell about it. That's a miracle in itself!

When we see a clown being shot out of a cannon at the circus, we laugh because we know it's not reality. When we're the ones being shot out or shot at, however, it's no laughing matter. It can be a thanksgiving matter, though. Not about what's happening to us, but for who protects us in the line of fire. When we take refuge in God, he promises us peace beyond human comprehension. Every situation is included. So don't be afraid. There's no battle too fierce for God!

> The LORD is my light and my salvation—whom shall I
>   fear?
> The LORD is the stronghold of my life—of whom shall I
>   be afraid?
> When evil men advance against me to devour my flesh,
> when my enemies and my foes attack me, they will
>   stumble and fall.
> Though an army besiege me, my heart will not fear;
> though war break out against me, even then will I be
>   confident. . . .
> Teach me your way, O LORD; lead me in a straight path
>   because of my oppressors.
> Do not turn me over to the desire of my foes,
> for false witnesses rise up against me, breathing out
>   violence.
> I am still confident of this:
> I will see the goodness of the LORD in the land of the
>   living.
> Wait for the LORD; be strong and take heart and wait
>   for the LORD. (Psalm 27: 1–3, 11–14) ☆

His Everlasting Arms
by BARBARA JOHNSON

I cried,
Lord, I'm so afraid tonight.
There's no rest for my soul.
Besieged by worry, fear, and pain,
I tossed and turned and rolled.
I prayed,
Lord, send your angel,
Someone to hold my hand,
Someone to touch my broken heart
And say, "I understand."
I prayed,
Lord, send a candle
To light this long, dark night,
A flame to warm and cheer me,
To set my soul aright.
I prayed,
Lord, send . . .
Then, that was all.
For what He sent to me
Was peace.
His everlasting arms
Carried me off
To sleep.

Ann Luna

Part 4

God's Outrageous Hope

No Contortions or Distortions

by PATSY CLAIRMONT

Every circus goer loves a good laugh, which is why I'm sure we have such a rollicking good time with those zany fun mirrors. You know, the ones in which we look either twelve feet high and two inches thick or we appear twelve feet wide and two inches high. I think it would be a hoot to slip some of those tricky mirrors into Marilyn, Luci, Sheila, Barbara, and Thelma's dressing rooms. Honk!

Seeing an exaggeration of ourselves is fun ... as long as it doesn't come too close to the truth. 'Cause the truth is hard enough to swallow without some clown (honk!) magnifying it. Therein lies the problem with mirrors—they are way too reflective. Somehow seeing things so, so ... *clearly* erases all hopes of distorting the visible truth. Then who's left laughing?

I'm grateful that our hope in Christ goes far beyond what we see in a mirror. Whew! Otherwise we would become people of despair. I mean, do you watch the evening news? Yikes! Now there's a scary mirror. Talk about a world full of distortions and contortions, in which humankind often appears wrenched and wretched. If the news programs truly mirror our society's shape, we had better take another look, because it's not too funny: children shooting children, rampant brutality, pervasive dishonesty, war atrocities, killer storms, moral decay, dismal predictions … Hey, would some-body send out for popcorn? This clown is starting to feel depressed! (Popcorn is Barbara's husband's favorite food, which he consumes in large quantities in good times and bad.)

Actually, depression is one of the results of distortion. Trust me, I know. I spent several years as a dismal prisoner in my home. You can bet I wasn't turning somersaults and cart-wheels in those days. My outlook on life had become so warped that, as Shakespeare said, "Every bush became a bear." I viewed myself through the distortion of fear, and believe me, fear both contorts and distorts. Like a contor-tionist who ties himself up in knots, I allowed fear to twist me in its exaggerated perspective. My snarled emotions then kept me from embracing the truth that in Christ I had "a future and a hope." Instead of my faith buoying my spirit like a bouquet of circus balloons caught in a summer breeze, I dragged my saggy beliefs around as if they were a bagful of rocks. That is, until I began to view myself through the liber-ating reflection of God's Word. The Bible is a hope-full mir-ror that, yes, exposes the truth about yesterday and today, but not without improving our outlook on tomorrow.

My friends have also been hope bearers for me by reflect-ing Christ's love both in my early years of struggle and today. For the past few years my Women of Faith comrades, Mari-lyn, Thelma, Sheila, Barbara, and Luci, have been like zany mirrors for me in that they assure me that my cockeyed reflection is both accurate and acceptable. They know this from having accepted their own wobbly conditions. What a relief! Yes, I am irregular in many ways, but the Lord is not surprised by the shape I'm in nor is he put off by my teeter-ing style or that of my friends.

Here's the best news from the Good News: Jesus eliminated distortions through the contortion of the cross. His twisted and broken body offered as a sacrifice for all has given us new reflective hope. Instead of seeing ourselves through our hopeless human condition, we have been given a divine perspective with an everlasting future. Jesus breaks the cords that bind us; he actually sets captives (even homebound clowns) free. Now that's outrageous! Balloons for everyone; I'm buying! Oh, I love a happy ending, especially when I get to be part of it. Honk! Honk!

Hark! Is that the band I hear? Why, yes, and what is it playing? That wonderful old hymn, "Whispering Hope." And no one loves music more than our next threesome, Luci, Thelma, and Sheila. You should hear them backstage harmonizing. Sometimes they even let Marilyn and me join in . . . if we whisper. So come along and join our team as they sing, whisper, and shout about hope until the big top billows. Oh, yes, and Barbara, who during her school days was known for playing a saw between her knees, will intersperse a few sweet notes of hope of her own. Trust me, this is one concert you won't want to miss. ☆

Let's Run Away and Join the Circus!

by LUCI SWINDOLL

My suitcase came off the shelf so fast it would've made your head swim. I was wildly throwing stuff in it when my father walked by the door and asked what I was doing.

"I've had it," I told him flatly. "Mother gives me way too much to do, my homework is too long and boring, my friends don't understand me, and God's too busy to know I'm even down here. I'm running away."

He ambled in, sat down on my bed, and asked if he could help me pack.

Well, s-h-o-o-o-t. I didn't want that. In all my little twelve-year-old fury, I dumped the contents of the bag on the bed and ran outside. I'd show Daddy. I wouldn't run away after all, and he'd just have to put up with my lousy attitude. So there!

Haven't you felt like that a hundred times? *I'm outa here! I don't have to live in this house. You've seen me for the last time. I'm moving. I want out of this family. Forever.* I certainly have. I don't so much anymore, but that's only because I live alone, and if I ran away I'd have to take me with me. (It's like my codependent friend who says that when she gets to the end of her rope, she imagines herself saying to her family, "Get in the car. I'm running away!")

There's no escaping reality, but we all try in a million different ways. Some of us sublimate, others ignore, and many (like me) live in denial. I told Marilyn the other day, "Denial is my reality." She laughed, but there's truth in that and she knows it. There are numerous times when living in the present is way too difficult, even though I am completely committed to the concept and preach it every chance I get. Like almost everything, it's easier said than done.

My mother used to say, "I'll be so glad when you kids are grown so I can quit making all these lunches." (Don't you know there were many days in our adult years when she thought, "I'd love to make lunch for those kids today.") Family responsibility is what Erma Bombeck referred to as "kids and car pools" and Lily Tomlin called "the world of meatballs and mending." Sameness gets old in a hurry.

In Anne Tyler's wonderful novel, *Ladder of Years*, the daily demands were getting to Delia Grinstead. She felt trapped, used by her husband and children, and tired of the mediocrity of her life. So, while on vacation with her family one summer, she walked away. Casually she meandered down the beach and wandered off. Way off. She found a new town, started a new job, took on a new name, and began a new life. She disappeared from her old life and started over.

Within a matter of months, however, she was back where she started—feeling trapped, used, and mediocre. She changed her circumstances, but her temperament and personality stayed the same; therefore, she did little more than re-create a reality similar to the one she'd supposedly escaped. As a critic said in his review of the book, "It just proves that knowing what you're tired of is not the same as knowing what you want." Delia Grinstead learned that the hard way.

Most of us know what we *don't* want in life, but not so many of us know what we *do* want. And not having what we want, or not wanting what we have, leads to discontentment, if not hopelessness and despair. But I've learned that there are ways around these feelings. We can run away, as Delia did. We can keep accumulating—things, people, experiences—trying to find what we *might* want, what's missing. We can learn to pretend that we're completely-satisfied-thank-you. Or . . . we can do the one and only thing that works: turn to God and his Word. It is he who brings about real change in our lives. And how does he do that? By giving us hope.

The person who has a relationship with the God of the universe, through his Son Jesus Christ, can know for sure that his hope is secure. It will not come up short. In fact, Paul tells us in Romans 5:2–5, "And we rejoice in the hope of the glory of God. Not only so, but we also rejoice in our sufferings, because we know that suffering produces perseverance; perseverance, character; and character, hope. And hope does not disappoint us, because God has poured out his love into our hearts by the Holy Spirit, whom he has given us."

There's a stick-to-itiveness about those words, isn't there? One thing leads to another, then another, and another . . . on and on. Like life. Banking on his infallible Word is the only way I know to deal with my imperfect life in this deteriorating world.

I learned that from my mother. She had a way of making Scripture very practical, and it proved life changing. For example, she held tremendous hope for all three of her children, and her hope came straight from Scripture: "A man's gift maketh room for him, and bringeth him before great men" (Proverbs 18:16 KJV). She wrote that verse on a three-by-five card and taped it above her kitchen sink. "I'm claiming this for my three children," she told my brother one day. While Babe and Orville and I fought over baseballs, household chores, and who ate the last popsicle, Mother was praying about our futures. She was believing God's promise that our various gifts would give us opportunities to minister to people "of importance," as the *Living Bible* puts it. Her hope for that outcome wasn't in her children (at the moment, we were giving her little hope); her hope was in God's faithfulness to his Word.

Mother also scribbled little comments in hymnbooks, and one day after she died I was leafing through the pages of one and found a hymn she had highlighted years before. I was amazed at verse four of "O Zion, Haste":

> *Give of thy sons to bear the message glorious;*
> *Give of thy wealth to speed them on their way;*

Pour out thy soul for them in prayer victorious;
And all thy spending Jesus will repay.

Mother was proactive about every word of that verse. She had two sons and gave them both to the ministry of Jesus Christ. She supported them with monetary gifts. She prayed for them. Today, both of my brothers are in Christian work, and have been all their adult lives. They minister to everyone, including people "of importance." Scripture promised it. Mother believed it. God brought it to pass. She was serious about hoping in Christ, and her prayer life proved it.

My mother was not a saint. I'm sure there were days when she even wanted to run away. But she learned how to rely on the ever-present grace of God, putting her faith constantly in him, holding fast to a hope that did not disappoint. I don't know why her children did the very thing she longed for them to do—certainly not because she did everything right all the time. My guess is simply that God answered her prayer. Her example of hoping in him makes me want to hang on, too, to the goodness of the God who loves me, regardless of the dailiness of life and my own frailties.

But what does that really look like? you might wonder. When your precious teenager is addicted to drugs or your best friend is mad at you or your four-year-old is driving you crazy with her center-stageism, where does hope come in? Let me suggest three practical ways to make it real in your life. I saw these principles incarnated in my mother's life, I've tested them again and again in my own, and I've watched many others bank on them as well.

Accept your reality.

Amy Carmichael says, "In acceptance lieth peace." Solomon advises us to accept what God has given us as a gift: "To enjoy your work and to accept your lot in life—that is indeed a gift from God" (Ecclesiastes 5:19 LB).

During the years I worked for Mobil Oil Corporation, there were numerous times I wanted to leave. Quit. Give it up and find a job that had more personal or spiritual gratification. But I believed God had put me in that environment for a purpose. It wasn't that I didn't like the company or that I didn't have any friends there, but there was a lack in my spirit that seemed constant—a plaguing sense that my daily activities had no eternal value.

I kept asking the Lord to open new doors for me and give me victory over those feelings of discontentment. Finally, after many years, I accepted the fact that God wanted me to work for Mobil and to stay until he moved me for his own good reasons. Peace came to me when I stopped fighting. I stayed with Mobil for thirty years, and I have never regretted it. The financial savings I started there grew to a nest egg that enables me to have a very comfortable retirement (if that time ever comes!). The professional growth and experience of those years have helped me in decision making, goal setting, and general maturing. And friends? To this day, those with whom I worked are among the most precious ones in my life. In fact, two of them travel with me almost everywhere I speak.

I don't know anybody who loves what she does or where she is every minute of the day. But the reality is, we are where we are, and God is doing something right there, whether we see it or not. He wastes nothing. He's growing us up in himself.

Bring God into your reality.

Bringing God into your reality means being fully present in the moment—not wishing you were somewhere you used to be or somewhere you hope to be. My dear friend Ney Bailey helps me bring God into my reality (and keep him there) by encouraging me to let my current anxieties be the springboard for praying specifically. In other words, when I'm worried about something, have financial troubles or relationship problems—whatever—I let that troublesome thing be the catalyst for talking to God in straightforward detail. I don't skirt what's bugging me. I don't act like it doesn't exist. I don't go on to other things. Right in the middle of my anxiety, I tell God about it, as if he were my dad.

Ney also says, "Luci, don't edit your prayers." I absolutely love that thought. When a child pulls at his mother's coattail for something he wants, he doesn't stand there thinking, *Now, how should I phrase this . . . let's see. Shall I start with "I want," or is that too forward?* Goodness, no! The kid blurts out his thoughts spontaneously, with total abandon. The sincerity of his heart exposes his deepest desires, petitions, and longings to the parent he loves and trusts. Praying that way to our heavenly Father fosters a bonding that's sweet and comforting.

Make life an adventure.

Would you believe that at the age of sixty-two, I took out a thirty-year loan and bought my first home? Why not? After all, I could still be going strong at ninety-two! Never, ever would I have dreamed that at this time in my life I'd be traipsing all over the country with a bunch of rowdy women, speaking to tens of thousands. What ever happened to retirement? And yet, with the new task God has set before me, he

has given me new hope for something for which I pray and
wait: trusting him to turn the world upside down through
the Women of Faith movement. To be a part of it is just icing
on the cake.

You're never too old to start living fully. Ask God for a
fresh perspective on your life. Try things you've never tried
before. Enlist in a joint project with friends—even with
people you don't know. Neighbors. Church buddies. Ask
yourself what you want most from life, and go for it. You
probably can't get it for yourself, but you can pray about it.
My brother Chuck says, "Hope doesn't require a massive
chain where heavy links of logic hold it together. A thin wire
will do . . . just strong enough to get us through the night
until the winds die down." Hope is a heartfelt assurance that
our heavenly Father knows what's best for us and never
makes a mistake. God says, "Trust me. Remember my Word.
Believe . . . and wait."

Of course, our greatest hope lies waiting for us at the end
of time, when all God's purposes will be fulfilled. We will go
to live with Jesus Christ, who by his grace redeemed us,
loved us through our trials, provided joy in the midst of
heartache, peace for our troubled hearts, and freedom from a
boring lifestyle. We'll be with him forever—an outrageous
reality!

The nineteenth-century poet Francis Thompson wrote
"The Hound of Heaven," the autobiography of a fugitive who
ran all his life from the redemptive love of God. Throughout
the poem, this glorious "Hound," who will not let Thompson alone, stays in hot pursuit. Thompson flees from him,
hides from him, fears him, pleads with him . . . fearing all the
while that if he lets his heart go, his own dreams will be

unfulfilled. Yet, unknowingly, the very thing for which he is searching is God himself. He has put his hope in everything but God, and been disappointed each time.

Finally, at the end of the poem, God gets his attention with these words:

Whom wilt thou find to love ignoble thee
Save Me, save only Me?
All which I took from thee I did but take,
Not for thy harms,
But just that thou might'st seek it in My arms.
All which thy child's mistake
Fancies as lost, I have stored for thee at home;
Rise, clasp My hand, and come!

Your mundane, everyday, tiresome life may seem like it isn't going anywhere, but believe me . . . it is. So don't run away and join the circus—as fun as it might be for a while! Take it from Delia Grinstead: "Real life" eventually sets in, and then you need more than wishful thinking to see you through. Thankfully, Christ offers all of us a sustaining hope in the midst of the here and now. Joy and fulfillment are not in another town, another job, another life. They're in your very own heart. Believe it. Clasp his hand and come. ☆

The Big Picture

by BARBARA JOHNSON

My friend Sue once wanted to run away after she blundered so terribly that she expected to be banned from her son's school forever.

Sue, a devoted parent-volunteer, used the PTA's new circus-style popcorn machine to treat her son's fourth-grade class to a popcorn party when the teacher said the class had earned a reward. Unfortunately, when she set up the popper in the hallway outside the classroom, she unknowingly parked it right under a heat sensor. Fifteen minutes later, the popcorn started popping, the fire alarms went off, and the whole school—all 437 students—evacuated.

And did I mention it was November? And raining cats and dogs?

When the principal came galloping down the hallway, he pointed to the heat sensor flashing above the popcorn popper and yelled, "Do you know what you've done?" That's when Sue knew she had to run away. She was sure those students and their teachers would never forgive her for sending them out into a driving rainstorm.

She was still in hiding a few days later, vowing never to show her face at the school again, when the principal called. "Come on back," he said.

"Never," Sue replied.

"Quit focusing on this one incident and look at the big picture," he said. "I forgive you—and the kids thought it was great. They love getting out of class, even if it means standing out in the rain."

"Really?" Sue asked.

"Of course," he said. "In fact, Miss Smith's kindergartners have earned a reward. I thought you might give them a popcorn party—in the cafeteria."

The next week, Sue opened the school's storeroom where the popcorn cart was parked. It took a moment to realize why it looked different. On top, someone had added a red light, the kind that flashes on top of emergency vehicles. And hanging from one of the cart's handles was a little firefighter's helmet with her name hand-lettered on the front. She looked at that popcorn cart and did something she wouldn't have believed a few days earlier. She laughed.

Sue's story always reminds me of the role hope plays in our lives. When we have hope, we can look at the big picture—God's promise of eternal life—rather than focus on our mistakes. When seen from that perspective it's easy to see that no matter what happens to us—or what havoc we unintentionally wreak on others—we will be able to learn from our mistakes and start over. We'll even be able to do what we never thought we could do: laugh again. ☆

Chapter 11

Get Your Hopes Up

by THELMA WELLS

I remember taking my children to the circus years ago. Each of us entered the big top with our own set of expectations. Having never been to the circus before, my kids didn't know quite what to expect, but I'm sure they had their own ideas of what they hoped to see. As for me, I just hoped my three little clowns wouldn't out-clown the real ones. I hoped they wouldn't have to use the bathroom more than once during the performance. And I hoped they'd make it through the afternoon without spilling soft drinks all over themselves (and me). Most of all, I hoped the big top experience would be worth all the money I'd spent.

When the show started and the lion tamer started showing off his ability to control the wild beast of the jungle, I hoped the big cat would not slap him down with one of those big paws. When the trapeze artists turned one bar loose to catch another bar in midair, I hoped they wouldn't fall, that their timing would be perfect—and that the whole event would be over soon. I got so uptight watching them then that I can feel the anxiety now, just thinking about it.

I was equally nervous when the tightrope walkers performed. Why in the world would anybody in their right mind want to balance themselves on a piece of rope suspended fifty feet above the ground? I can imagine several reasons. One, they are completely crazy. Two, they are awfully desperate for money and this is the only job they can get. Three, they get a serious thrill from risking their lives. Whatever their reason, I just hoped they wouldn't fall. I'm certain they hoped for a successful performance as well, but all the hope in the world can't prevent a mishap once in a while.

That's the way life is. We bounce into life not really knowing what to expect. When we're very young, we're full of excitement about all our "firsts"—our first steps, our first day of school, our first circus! And if we're surrounded by super healthy, faith-filled adults, then we get the message, "Get ready for the exciting and wonderful time you'll have watching and participating in the events of your life!" But most of us don't get that message, do we? Instead we're warned, "Don't get your hopes up." Don't expect too much—you'll only be disappointed.

During the first quarter of 1998, all of the speakers for the Women of Faith conference had been sick with colds or respiratory ailments, except for me. Around the end of the quarter I starting saying things to myself like, "I hope I don't get sick . . . We've been traveling so much and have been around so many different people, I hope I don't get some of the stuff they might have . . . I hope I don't get a sore throat . . . I hope I don't catch a cold." The thought of getting sick was on my mind so strongly that I started thinking I was feeling bad. All my negative wishful thinking finally came true: the week before Easter I was thoroughly ill with a cold, sore throat, fever, everything I'd "hoped" not to have.

My doctor examined me and prescribed a remedy. I'm sure it was working in a timely manner, but it was not working fast enough for me. Guess what happened? I panicked. I thought, "I can't be sick! I've got to speak next week. I've got to get well quick." So, the infamous "Dr. Thelma Wells" decided to add to the doctor's prescription. I overmedicated myself and got sicker than sick. I could hardly raise my head off the pillow because it was throbbing so bad.

Naturally, I thought that adding another over-the-counter medication for my headache would be a good idea. WRONG! With so many drugs on the warpath in my body, they all ran into each other and created more chaos than ever. My head was still throbbing, I was nervous and shaking, my equilibrium was off, my speech was slurred . . . I was a mess!

Easter Sunday came and I was still as sick as could be. My house was filled with my annual Easter weekend visitors, but I couldn't lift a finger to be hospitable. Everybody had gone to church except me, and I was indulging in a major pity party because this was the first time in my whole life that I'd missed church on Easter Sunday.

As I lay in bed bemoaning my plight, the Holy Spirit turned my spiritual light on. Suddenly I got mad! I sat up in bed, made my way to the couch in the living room, and started talking to myself in a different way than I had during the first three months of the year. I began to denounce the defeating, lying, tricky spirit that caused me to think myself into the state I was in. Not only had I "hoped" myself into a cold and sore throat, but my fear that I wouldn't get well fast enough drove me to act out of desperation and defeat the prescription medication that was already working for me. I had allowed the spirit of fear to impede my progress.

God's Word tells us that the spirit of fear is not from God, but from our enemy, the devil. So I started rebuking the enemy within and focusing on the only real hope I have: Christ Jesus, the hope of glory. I told Satan that I resist him, and his spirit of fear was to come out of me this instant! I repented before God and told him how sorry I was that I hadn't recognized what was happening to me when I was panicking and taking matters into my own hands. I asked for forgiveness. I didn't "hope" he forgave me; I stood on his Word that when we ask for forgiveness, he will instantly grant it. I started singing the words of a hymn: "My hope is built on nothing less than Jesus' blood and righteousness." I affirmed before God that my only hope was in him. I told him, "My hope is so strong that I expect you to heal me today."

This singing and praying went on for the rest of the morning. I began to feel a little better, but my head was still pounding and I was still having difficulty balancing my steps. Later, when everybody got home from church and we'd prayed over the Easter meal, my daughters, Lesa and Vikki, called me into the bedroom while others were filling their plates with food. My girls put their hands on me and prayed for me again, rebuking Satan, speaking healing to my spirit, canceling the plans the enemy had for me. They acted just like the elders of the church—only the anointing oil was missing.

When they finished praying for me, I went into the kitchen, fixed my plate, and ate heartily even though I still felt a bit out of sorts. God the Healer heard our prayers. He responded to my attitude change as I moved from wishing I'd be all right to expecting to be well. He knew that I'd finally distinguished between hoping and Hoping. My confidence had been placed in the only one who cannot lie, disappoint, or renege on a promise. Before the evening ended, my head had stopped throbbing, my throat was no longer sore, my balance was corrected, I was back to my old self. The spiritual surgery God had performed on my soul had opened the door to physical healing in my body.

I'm sure you have plenty of your own stories that showcase God's faithfulness. God has proved himself over and over in our lives; our hope in him is never empty. But when our minds start swinging from one negative thought to another like an acrobat flying from one trapeze to the next, we find ourselves in danger of falling. The trapeze artist who loses concentration can easily miss connecting with her partner or the swinging bar. Yikes! Down on the net she goes. She may be embarrassed or a little shaken, but most of the time she is not seriously injured.

Jesus is like that net. He is always beneath us, waiting to catch us when we lose our concentration on him and miss the connection. He's our only real H.O.P.E.

H: Heavenly.

O: Omnipotent.

P: Powerful.

E: Everlasting Savior.

When we trust in him alone, life may still shake us up, but our spirit will be safe in the net of his love.

Many of us have ideas about hope that are simply all wrong—totally contrary to what biblical hope is all about. Either we experience hope as mere wishful thinking ("I hope I lose weight"—when we ain't doin' a thing about it), or we cynically dismiss it as child's play ("Now that I have some life experience under my belt, I know it's foolish to hope for things I'm never gonna get anyway").

As born-twice, Holy-Spirit-filled women of God, we can do better! Hope for the Christian is much more than pie-in-the-sky wishful thinking. The dictionary defines hope as a verb of expectation—to "hope against hope," to actively and confidently expect fulfillment. Hope as a noun is defined as a confident expectation that a desire will be fulfilled. Hope as a virtue is described as the confidence with which a Christian looks for God's grace in this world and glory in the next. Colossians 1:27 affirms that the most glorious mystery of all is "Christ in you, the hope of glory."

Did you get the common denominator? Hope is all about placing our confidence in what we can't yet see, about having high expectations that, in spite of all appearances to the contrary, our deepest longings will be fulfilled. And as Christians, that's exactly what we can count on. Psalm 39:7 says, "And now, Lord, what do I wait for and expect? My hope and expectation are in You" (AMPLIFIED). And there's Psalm 62:5: "My soul, wait only upon God and silently submit to Him; for my hope and expectation are from Him" (AMPLIFIED). The only hope we have is in Christ Jesus!

My personal message of hope involves an outrageous metaphor, the bumblebee. Over twenty years ago I learned that bumblebees are outrageous because they shouldn't be able to fly, but they do anyway. Their bodies are too heavy and their wingspan is too shallow, but because God is in charge of both bumblebees and aeronautical science, he has enabled bees to defy the laws of aerodynamics. That's what hope is all about: having the confidence that despite your personal limitations and circumstances, God has filled you with his Spirit so you can defy the odds and accomplish his perfect will for your life.

When I struggled with my marriage and feared it would end in disaster, I had a living hope inside my soul that kept me going forward and straining for those glimpses of success that encouraged me to "keep on hoping, keep on praying, keep on trusting." I was so young when I married—only twenty. My husband was seven years my senior and a real "man of the world." Like a lot of women, I believed in the fairy tales that end "... and they lived happily ever after." Little did I know that "happily" would not last a lifetime for me.

It was not many years after that blissful wedding day that I discovered every woman's worst nightmare: my husband was having an affair. Things weren't pretty around my house for several years. I considered my options: separation, divorce, homicide. But in my heart of hearts, I knew that God had joined us together. You see, when I was fourteen years old I started praying for God to send me a godly husband—one I could live happily ever after with. When I saw this man at church, I knew he was the one. After six years of friendship and dating, we were married on April 1, 1961. I refused to believe that I had been April Fooled.

Of course I was hurt, disappointed, disgusted, traumatized, angry, disillusioned, paranoid. Sometimes I was violent,

I often fussed and brought up his sin, I cried a lot, beat myself up, loved my husband one moment and hated him the next. Strangely, however, I still had hope. My natural self told me to leave him; my spirit said stay. Sometimes my granny would act as my spiritual conscience and I'd hear her voice in my mind: "Keep hope alive. Get your hopes up for this situation to end. Keep your hope in Jesus alone—only he can fix this mess so you can live happily ever after."

But one day my natural self got a burr in its saddle sharp enough to convince me it was time to tell my husband to hightail it out of the house. I was ready to give him a divorce and be done with it. I gave him three days to get out.

Early on that third morning, a deacon of our church and his wife telephoned us. They said they didn't know anything about what was happening in our house, but God had prompted them to call us and pray for deliverance and restoration in our marriage. When they'd finished praying and we'd all hung up, my husband and I were silent for a long time. He finally spoke these words through tear-filled eyes: "Thelma, I've mistreated you. I've done everything to you that a person could do. You did not deserve it. You have been the best wife anyone could ask for. I promise you that from now on, I will never deliberately do anything to hurt you. It's over. I want you. Will you please forgive me?"

My heart was pounding. I couldn't stop crying. But through my tears I accepted my husband's apology and gave him another chance. Somehow I had known that a divorce was not the answer for us. The hope I had clung to, the confidence I had in God's Word that nothing should put our marriage asunder, had enabled me to "fly anyway"—to defy the odds and, like the bumblebee, keep on doing what I was called to do even when everything seemed stacked against me. God answered the prayers of my friends and gave my husband and me the willingness to be restored and reconciled to each other. It's been nearly three decades since that fateful morning, and I can truly say, life began again "... and they lived happily ever after."

You, too, can keep on keeping on when you put your hope in God alone. You can get your hopes up and keep them up as you walk on the tightropes of life. You can swing from one trapeze bar to the next when you are confident in your hope that even if you fall, as the flying trapeze artists sometimes do, there is a net of protection under you that prevents your ultimate destruction.

This kind of sustaining hope is rooted in faith—in the steadfast assurance that what God has revealed and promised in his Word is true. We grab onto this hope when we fly out in faith, believing that God will do what he says. We find the confidence to fly by remembering how God has kept his promises to us in the past, analyzing how he is keeping them in the present, and believing that he will do no less in the future.

I recently heard hope described so vividly by my pastor, Barry John Lyons, Sr. He said that people who have a relationship with Jesus and who understand the implications of their salvation through him can rest in their hope like babes in arms. Salvation is three-dimensional, he said: past, present, future. In the past we were saved from the penalty of sin; in the present we are saved from the power of sin; in the future we will be saved from the punishment of sin. When we repent, believe, and receive Jesus Christ as our personal Savior, we are justified, found "not guilty" in the sight of

God. Then we are sanctified, one day at a time, as the Holy Spirit within us changes our hearts and we respond by doing more right than wrong. When we die we will be glorified, never to hope for more! We will finally be at home in hope, forever.

Hope is a precious gift of our salvation. According to Hebrews 6:19, "we have this hope as an anchor for the soul, firm and secure." While we can "hope" that circus performers don't fall and that our kids don't spill their soda, we must remember that our only reliable hope is in what we cannot see or control: the outrageous faithfulness of God. Our responsibility to him as his children is to study his character so we will know, without a doubt, that whatever way he deals with our circumstances in life, it's the right way. Even when things don't work out the way we planned or desired, he is all-knowing, all-loving, the beginning and the ending. Hope is acting on the conviction that despite what we see with the natural eye, God is working in the spiritual realm to accomplish his perfect will in our lives. His hope does not disappoint!

God's Word declares hope. God's promises proclaim hope. We must think hope. Speak hope. Pray hope. Sing hope. Act out hope. Stand firm on hope. Share hope. In other words, get our hopes up. Because hope has been given to us, we can expect the best, even in the worst conditions. Praise God! ☆

Getting Up for the Finish
by BARBARA JOHNSON

Someone once said, "There are no hopeless situations—only people who are hopeless about them." Bonnie St. John Deane learned that truth firsthand in the 1984 Disabled Olympics.

In the first run down the slalom course, she soundly beat her closest competitor, a skier from Austria. She confidently expected to finish first again on the second run and win the medal. Instead she fell on a patch of ice. Greatly disappointed, Bonnie halfheartedly stood up and finished the course.

The Austrian won the gold medal—but not for skiing a flawless course. In fact, she, too, slipped and fell. She won gold, "not for skiing faster but for getting up faster," Bonnie wrote in her book, *Succeeding Sane*. From that experience Bonnie learned that "winners aren't people who never make mistakes. Winners are those who get up and finish. Gold-medal winners get up the fastest."

What a powerful analogy of the difference hope makes in our lives! Hope gives us a confident attitude that helps us get back up if we should fall. It injects us with a healthy dose of joy that assures us that no matter what happens to us on the course of life, we do not "grieve like the rest of men, who have no hope" (1 Thessalonians 4:13). Hope is the fuel that reminds us to "be strong and do not give up, for your work will be rewarded" (2 Chronicles 15:7). And finally, it is the reason we can "rejoice in our sufferings, because we know that suffering produces perseverance; perseverance, character; and character, hope. And hope does not disappoint us" (Romans 5:3–5).

Chapter 12

The Biggest Big Top

by SHEILA WALSH

Barry and I never have time to go to the movies anymore. We're on the road so much, and when we're home I'd rather take Christian to the park, or we all get into our jammies and watch "Frosty the Snowman." But last week was different. Barry's mom and dad asked if Christian could go home to Charleston with them for four days. I was in agony, but Marilyn Meberg convinced me that he would be fine. (Actually, I knew Christian would be fine; it was me I was worried about!)

On our second free night we looked at the paper to see if there was anything interesting playing, and I was thrilled to see that *Simon Birch* was still showing. I had loved the book

159

the movie is based on, John Irving's *A Prayer for Owen Meany*. Friends who had already seen the film advised me to take a full box of Kleenex, so with tissues in tow Barry and I set off.

The movie tells the story of a boy who is born with severe abnormalities. He is tiny, his best friend carries him around in a small basket attached to his bike, and his parents, perhaps out of superstition or fear, reject him. But Simon is a boy with an acute sense of destiny. He knows that God has put him on earth for a reason, and he is determined to fulfill his purpose.

Simon believes that God has called him to be a hero. Everyone looks at him and laughs, but it doesn't matter to Simon because there is a stronger melody playing in his spirit. And then his heroic moment comes: when he is just twelve years old, he dies saving the lives of a school bus full of children.

I could hear people all around me in the theater sobbing into their tissues, but I didn't need mine. I wanted to stand up and shout "Hallelujah!" Obviously I wasn't happy that a wonderful young boy had died, but I was thrilled for him because he "got it." He saw clearly that this life we cling to, frantically squeezing every ounce of pleasure out of it as if we are dying of thirst, is not "it." Simon had lived his life, fulfilled his God-given mission, and now he was home. He knew that his life on earth was just the beginning.

When I was twenty-three and working for Youth for Christ in England, I had a day off in a city called Colchester. I asked the couple I was staying with what was the most fun thing to do in their fair city, and they told me I simply had to see the zoo. Well, I'm not a huge zoo fan; the animals always look so bored and fed up. But my hosts made such a fuss about their jolly zoo that I decided to check it out.

The only reasonable conclusion I could come to is that they don't get out much. It was the worst zoo I've ever seen in my life! There were about three animals, and one of them looked like it had been dead for two weeks but no one had noticed. The aquarium was a tank of fish in a hut with a handwritten sign "The much feared pirrana" (spelled wrong!). I laughed so hard that I definitely got my money's worth.

I sometimes feel that way about our seventy allotted years: we build it up as if this is it, but it's not. All of us need to keep our faces lifted up toward Home because there is a day coming that will put all our best moments and our worst nightmares into the fires of forgetfulness. This is our glorious, outrageous hope: There is a day coming! "Never again will they hunger; never again will they thirst. The sun will not beat upon them, nor any scorching heat. For the Lamb at the center of the throne will be their shepherd; he will lead them to springs of living water. And God will wipe away every tear from their eyes" (Revelation 7:16–17).

What is your vision of heaven? What are you hoping for? I used to picture my life in eternity as . . . well, a bit dull. I mean, what would I do all day? Once I had chatted with all the great heroes of the faith and had a good look around to see who made it and who didn't, then what? Would it just be two million rounds of "Kum Ba Ya"? When I lined up my best hopes for down here and my best guesses about heaven, I decided that I'd better enjoy my life down here as much as possible before that great eternal chorus kicked in. Now don't get me wrong. I knew that the alternative was an eternity apart from God, which is unthinkable. But heaven just didn't sound very challenging to me.

I'm amazed that God doesn't just slap me around sometimes. I'm so small minded; I have the vision of a housefly. And yet in his grace and outrageous love he keeps talking to me and letting me in on the big picture. We are told that now we see through a glass darkly, but then we will see face-to-face. It's as if all our lives the only reflection we've had of ourselves and each other is the distorted image in a fun-house mirror; but when that day comes, the distorted images will be gone, everything crooked made straight, everything snapped back into place.

I was invited by my dear friend Joni Eareckson Tada to fly to Chicago and speak to her staff and major donors at their annual retreat. At the end of the weekend Joni and I carved out some alone time. As she talked about a new book project on heaven I found myself considering all the reasons why such a project would be appealing to her. I imagined her running through green fields after spending years in a wheelchair. I saw her lifting her arms to the sky, rubbing her own nose, stroking the face of her husband, combing her hair (do we still do that in heaven, and if so, will there be a place to plug in my hair dryer?).

Joni noticed me smiling so I let her in on the movie that had been running in my head. "Sounds great," she said. "But the real reason I'm longing for heaven is that I'm tired of sinning."

You could have knocked me over with a *Journey Into Life* tract! I know Joni to be one of the godliest women I have ever spent time with, and yet the reason she longed for heaven was so that her struggle with the flesh would be over.

I was stunned by her words. I was challenged by her awareness of her sinfulness. Too often I get so used to the jerk I am that I don't even notice anymore. And yet here was a woman who can't experience many of the normal things of everyday life, warring against her flesh as a wide-awake child of God. I told her as we parted that she put me to shame. She smiled at me and said, "Well, you know, Sheila, in many ways I'm a lot more blessed than you."

"What do you mean, Joni?" I asked.

"I can't ever forget that I'm disabled."

Wow! That's outrageous! Outrageously true. We're all disabled; it's just that some of us hide our disabilities on the inside. But there is a day coming when all of that will disappear in an instant. I can't imagine what that will be like. I can't conceive of perfect relationships—all our emotional baggage left behind. Think of the people in your life that you have the greatest struggle with. If they are fellow sons or daughters of God, then your relationship with them in the biggest Big Top of all will be as sweet as homegrown tomatoes. Outrageous!

As I reflected on Joni's words on my flight home, I took fresh joy in this outrageous hope that is ours in Christ. This is not wishful thinking, it is his promise to all who hope in him. "It is written: 'No eye has seen, no ear has heard, no mind has conceived what God has prepared for those who love him'" (1 Corinthians 2:9).

Only in the past few years have I begun to yearn for heaven. I'm beginning to see our lives down here so differently now. I think of it all as the tuning up of an orchestra before a great opera or concert begins. All the instruments are there, but no one is playing together. They're all doing their own little thing to make sure their instruments are in tune. You hear the French horns for a while, louder than the rest. Then it's the violins or the cellos. Then it's everyone at once, but not together. The cacophony definitely doesn't sound like music.

But for a moment all the individual sounds cease, and then the symphony begins. You are no longer aware of every individual player, but you hear the most glorious sound. Does that mean that all individuality is lost? Far from it. It just means that everyone is finally doing what they were created to do.

As children of God, we live as though we are tuning up for the show, waiting for the curtain to rise and our real lives to begin. With this outrageous hope for tomorrow, we can live with renewed passion for today.

But how does a vision of heaven affect how we live in the midst of bills to be paid, cancer to be fought, children to be raised? I think a new perspective of the bigger picture would change everything. I remember reading something that Corrie ten Boom shared with an audience that I found so helpful in my own life. She held up a piece of cloth to the crowd gathered before her and asked them what they saw. It wasn't very impressive. Threads ran in conflicting directions, and there was no clear picture or continuity to the piece. It was so knotted in places that it actually looked ugly. Then she turned it over. It was breathtaking. On the other side, the "right" side, was a beautiful crown embroidered in exquisite detail. What the audience had seen up until that point was only the mass of knotted threads on the back.

That's how I see things now. We're looking at our lives from the back, and all we can see are the knots where new thread was used and colors changed. What God sees is the other side. He sees what we are becoming—the beautiful picture he designed before the world began. What a hope! Not because any of us in our own strength could make anything even the dog would sit on, but because God is doing it. Right now, if all the knots of your life look ugly to you, take heart. God is making something you'll want to frame for eternity.

When I was twenty-two I knew so much. Now at forty-two I know very little. But the very little I know now is worth more to me than all the stuff I used to think was important. I know that God has not forgotten where I live. I know that not a moment of my life is wasted if I'll offer it up to him. I don't have tidy answers anymore for all the heartache that's in the world, but when I try to view life with an eternal perspective, I find hope even in the darkest corners.

I am no Pollyanna. I don't believe in burying my head in the sand. I like to face life head-on and deal with it. Having said that, I refuse to get caught up in the spirit of despair that is seeping through the world and creeping into the church. We look at world events, the economy, the chaos, and we become filled with fear of the days that lie ahead, as if God hadn't read the latest edition of *Time* magazine before he gave us his Word. But no matter what is going on around us, God is in control. He has not fallen off his throne and never will. Every moment of our lives is planned by God. He makes no mistakes. It's just that from this side of the cloth, we can't see the whole picture.

When I was working on my last album, "Hope," it was very important to me that every song contained this rich truth that God is weaving through the tapestry of my own life. I wanted my listeners to feel like I was sitting down with them, one at a time, hand in hand, and singing to them about the hope that does not disappoint. When you've been in a dark place and have lost hope, and into that solitary cell the Lamb of God has come to sit and weep with you, and then carried you out, you long to share that hope with others. Hope is no longer just in my head; it's written all over my heart. It has become as deep as the marrow in my bones.

> *You alone are the Savior of my heart*
> *Faithful in all you do*
> *You alone are the keeper of my soul*
> *Tender and kind and true.*
>
> *I will seek you in the morning*
> *I will seek your face at night*
> *How lovely is your presence to me, oh Lord, to me.*
>
> *Take my heart with all its wandering ways*
> *Shelter me in your grace*
> *There I'll stay till all my days are through*
> *Then I shall see your face.*

George Eliot wrote, "It's never too late to be what you might have been." For the believer this is not just one more faintly uttered New Year's resolution that looks over our shoulder like a disapproving teacher. It is our hope, our promise, our future. Hallelujah! ☆

Sideshow

Looking Around for God
by Barbara Johnson

As someone once said, hope is the feeling you have that the feeling you have isn't permanent! I find that especially comforting to remember when I'm flying on an airplane.

When the airplane suddenly dips and dances around the sky in a rift of turbulence, inevitably I find myself looking around for the flight attendants. It's not that I need to ask them to explain what's happening. I just need to see their faces. As the plane bounces through those invisible bumps several miles above the earth, I look into their eyes and almost always find calm reassurance. From their steady demeanor I conclude that even though it feels to me like we've just set out on Mr. Toad's Wild Ride, it's really nothing unusual. Their faces tell me the airplane is going to keep on flying no matter how bad the bumps are, and everything's going to be all right.

Now, I know this is just part of the flight attendants' professionalism. They know their passengers are studying them for signs of alarm, and they've been trained to show nothing but pleasant emotions. When I'm searching their faces for signs of hope, I try not to remember that fact! At that moment, I need to believe that what I see on their faces reflects reality, not their training!

Fortunately, for Christians there's no such ambiguity. When our lives get bumpy, we start looking around for God. It's not that we expect him to explain why things are happening the way they are (although occasionally we do whine, "Why me, Lord?"). We just need to remind ourselves that he is there, still in control. And everything's going to be all right—if not in this life, then certainly in the next!

As believers, when we look around for hope, we find God, constant and true. ☆

Part 5

God's
Outrageous
Freedom

Clowning Around

by PATSY CLAIRMONT

Ever watch those little cars pull under the big top, and a gazillion clowns tumble out the doors and windows? You know shenanigans are about to begin. Buckets full of confetti are pitched forward like so much cold water, hats hide hats that hide hats, and handkerchiefs the length of Connecticut spew forth from pockets. Clowns makes us feel giddy and kiddy. For a while we are young again, it's summer, and the horizon is full of helium balloons. In the presence of clowns, eating cotton candy as though it's from one of the five nutritional food groups suddenly makes sense. Honk! Honk!

Being a clownlike gal with my impish ways, I could be a little partial, but I think it's more than clowns' comical attire, their water-filled flowers, or their bulbous horns (honk!) that endear them to the world. I think the big appeal is their outrageous freedom to play the fool, the mime, the juggler, the victim, the hero, the keystone cop, or the lost waif. Yes, a clown can be whomever she chooses, not only without opposition but also to rousing applause.

While we tend to give circus clowns encores for their expressive freedom, we generally are not as generous with each other. In fact, it's not easy to be oneself without running into opposition. Rules, expectations, belief systems, and opinions can keep us mired in legalism and criticism. The good news is that Jesus came for clowns like us, to set us free from the clowns who would cast buckets full of stones in our direction. And stones are something Jesus was acquainted with. His personal freedom was an offense to many who wanted to pummel him with their hard-edged convictions, not to mention some pretty hefty rocks. The Pharisees' knotted beliefs kept them so bound to the law that they missed the love and therefore the Liberator.

At the Women of Faith conferences, we meet women who have suffered great losses and find themselves overwhelmed with grief. At times I wonder how they've had the strength and courage to get out of bed and make their way to a gathering. After the conference women will often come to us or write to tell us how something that was said was exactly what they needed to hear. They frequently use the word "freedom" in their correspondence, signifying God's liberating touch. They speak of the freedom of forgiveness, freedom from fears, freedom from people's opinions, and even the freedom to have a knee-slapping, sidesplitting, rip-roaring, good laugh.

One such letter came from a dear woman who had recently been widowed after thirty-five years of marriage. She was invited by a friend to attend a Women of Faith conference but was reluctant to come, and understandably so. Grief is such a taxing process, requiring so much of one physically and emotionally. But after a number of friendly nudges, she agreed to attend. She said that weekend she laughed deeply and well and couldn't believe the temporary liberation it afforded her from her pain. That laughing could offer her such sweet release fascinated her, so she began to study the benefits of a good giggle. In the process, she came across an ad for a clown school. Well, guess what?

Yep, she is now a bona fide clown. Honk! Honk! She performs at hospitals, parades, and private circuses (parties).

I love that story. This woman continues her journey of grief, but she brings healing laughter to others. Talk about freedom in the midst of crisis! Jesus liberates us, his people, that we might "stand fast" and not be disabled by the "yoke of bondage."

I have noticed that the more a person has experienced the liberating love and acceptance of Christ, the more freedom she can welcome in others. In the past few years, I have loved hanging out with my liberated joy friends Luci, Sheila, Marilyn, Thelma, and Barbara. They are outrageous, and I find that appealing. Don't misunderstand. We don't always agree, but we have enough inner freedom (honk!) to agree to disagree. No stone throwing here. (Well, perhaps an occasional pebble, which we backtrack to reclaim.)

In the following pages Barbara, Luci, Marilyn, and Thelma will do somersaults, handstands, back flips, and more if needed, to demonstrate the outrageous freedom available to us in Christ. So bring on the clowns (liberated joy givers) with their up-and-down smiles, their big flashy ties, and their hearts the size of a circus tent. And while you're at it, make my cotton candy a double. ☆

Goofy and Proud of It!

by LUCI SWINDOLL

Anybody who knows me knows I love a party. The more outrageous the better. The birthday of my friend Sid Wright proves this point.

Sid was born on New Year's Eve (of all times), and a couple years ago his wife, Ann, decided to give him a surprise party. Mary Graham and I were in charge of the evening's fun and games. One would think that with the proximity of Disney World (they all live in Orlando), the entertainment might be provided by a creative team from there. Not on your life! We called several of the invited guests and recruited them for the performance opportunity of a lifetime. (We only asked those who are a bit goofy.) No talent was required. All they needed was courage and a sense of the outrageous.

I can't remember when I had more fun than I did that night! One of the participants did a monologue she had learned forty years ago at summer camp, and another quoted a twisted version of a nursery rhyme: "Starkle, Starkle Little Twink." Someone tap-danced on a breadboard to the tune of that great old hymn of the faith, "Anchor's Aweigh," played on the trumpet. (That was especially meaningful since Sid is a retired naval captain.) I was interviewed as Sid's fictitious old flame, Inez, and did a rather provocative song and dance, if I do say so myself. A dear (and otherwise sophisticated) couple performed a country western duet, and the trio that closed the evening dazzled us with their uninhibited chore-ography. The pièce de résistance was a gorgeously decorated cake that caught fire. I'll tell you, from start to finish, the whole evening was hilarious. We laughed till we cried and couldn't get anybody to go home. Long after 2 A.M., I finally fell into bed as happy as a clam . . . and still laughing.

The very next morning, the phone started ringing. "You know, I could have done a great yo-yo act if you had asked me," one caller lamented. "Why didn't you let me know you wanted such classy entertainment?" Word was out that the best party of the year went down at Sid's place, and everyone wanted details on what they'd missed! Still others called to ask, "Do you travel around the country? We'd like your troupe to perform at our party. What do you charge?" Mary and I decided that we'd better be out of town every New Year's Eve from then on. Neither of us have enough faith to believe we can be Cecil B. DeMille more than once!

Anything funny, fresh, and free turns my crank, whether it's just for my own amusement and amazement or for a room full of people. That's one reason I love the circus. There's something outrageously free about death-defying acts and demonstrations of strength, courage, and derring-do. I'm captivated by the fact that something so hard can be made to look so easy.

Authors and poets have written about the circus; painters have captured on canvas or in sculpture circus acts, jugglers, tightrope walkers, trapeze artists, and harlequins. What is it that attracts us to these fetes of beauty and magic? I think it's the fact that the whole thing is incongruous, completely out of the ordinary, not captive to the natural laws of earth—free. We want to perform in the rather bizarre and surreal spectacle ourselves, but knowing we can't, we delight in watching others court danger and invert the status quo.

As Christians, however, I believe that we can do much more than live vicariously. The believer who chooses to live life on the cutting edge, risking everything for Christ's sake, can live the adventure Saint Augustine suggested: "Love God, and live as you please." Now, that's a scary thought. In fact, for most Christians it's radical, impossible, and revolutionary. Doesn't living as we please suggest utter rebellion, raw disobedience, and steely resistance to everything we know God wants of us?

Not for the grace-centered Christian. The one who knows for sure she has been set free by the redemptive work of Jesus Christ on the cross is the one who has conviction and strength of purpose to live by the power of the Holy Spirit rather than by the regulation of the law. She realizes that when a person loves God first and foremost, living as she pleases will be living to please him.

Christ was born under the law, kept the law, died under the law, and was the fulfillment of the law. By reconciling us to God, Christ has bought our freedom to live out of his marvelous grace instead of continuing to labor under a law no human being can ever follow perfectly. By making us righteous by his grace rather than through our own efforts, we are enabled to become more like him every day. I love that! The longer I walk with him, the more I understand that grace actually holds us to a much higher standard than the law ever required. Grace calls us to be like Jesus himself—in deed, word, and thought. Outrageous!

I was at a dinner party one night where we were all talking about what's wrong with the world. (Enjoyable little gathering.) Somebody said, "I think if people would just live by the Ten Commandments, all the world's problems would be solved." Someone else concurred: "Keeping the Ten Commandments is good enough for me." And another chimed in with, "I'm trying to memorize the Ten Commandments so I'll have them in my mind when I need them."

Oh, brother, I thought, *here we go.* (My brother Chuck told me he was in a meeting once where the speaker offered twenty dollars to the person in the audience who could quote the Ten Commandments by heart. He regretted he didn't know them so went straight home and committed all ten to memory. Then he added, "And you know, Sis, to this day nobody's ever offered me twenty bucks for the Ten Commandments.")

Clearing my throat and bucking up my courage, I said, "I couldn't disagree more." Heads turned, voices died down, everybody waited and stared. (I expected my hostess to say my cab had arrived.) But I went on boldly: "Why in the world would anybody want to live in bondage to the Ten

Commandments when Jesus Christ has set us free? Frankly, I choose freedom. I'd much rather live out of the richness of the book of Hebrews than try to keep the law of Exodus."

So there I was—the party pooper of the evening. I noticed the conversation quickly changed to the topics of salad dressing and good buys on panty hose. But I stick by my conviction. Now I'm not suggesting we take one book out of the Bible and ignore it because we prefer another book more; that would be ludicrous. But I know enough about Scripture to understand what Paul meant when he said we are not justified under the law but under grace; and I know enough about life to understand that only a fool would choose bondage over freedom.

Most Christians agree that we are saved by grace and grace alone. Paul makes it perfectly clear. But he's also clear about the fact that the way we mature in Christ is also by grace alone: "I have been crucified with Christ and I no longer live, but Christ lives in me. The life I live in the body, I live by faith in the Son of God, who loved me and gave himself for me" (Galatians 2:20). And Paul adds in Galatians 5:18: "But if you are led by the Spirit, you are not under law."

God sets us free from everything that would hold us to the earth so we can defy the bonds of the law and soar in freedom with him. Why don't Christians race to this truth, embrace it, and live the rest of their lives in freedom instead of in bondage? I believe it's because they don't trust themselves with grace. It seems too free, without strict guidelines. They don't quite know what to do without a bunch of rules that tell them exactly how to behave. I mean, what if they make a mistake? It's just too outrageous to them to think that God would trust them with this much freedom.

I certainly acknowledge the importance of the Ten Commandments in the scheme of God's economy, I rejoice in the fact they are part of the finished canon of Scripture, and I honor the principles they teach. I rejoice, however, that Jesus himself consolidated them into two commands: "'Love the Lord your God with all your heart and with all your soul and with all your mind and with all your strength.' The second is this: 'Love your neighbor as yourself.'" (Mark 12:30–31). Jesus knew we could do that only if the Spirit of God is controlling our lives. If he is, we'll fulfill the Ten Commandments. But try in our own power to keep them? We'll fail as miserably as the Israelites did.

There's something about being bound to a law or rule that makes us want to do the very opposite. Yet, when we have true freedom, we don't focus on the rules; we focus on Christ. Jesus teaches that we don't need regulations to keep us in line; rather, we need his love to control us. My brother sums it up well: "The wonderful thing about grace is that once it comes into our lives we are set free from a preoccupation with ourselves. Set free from the worry of whether we are doing enough to please God, we are free to serve him in love."

I've noticed that where grace abounds, people tend to rise to higher levels of trustworthiness. For example, when I worked at Mobil, my friend Ruth and I sometimes took an extended "hour" for lunch. We'd drive the ten miles into Los Angeles for hamburgers and fries at one of our favorite fun places. From there we'd head down Sunset Boulevard to "Famous Amos" for a bag of fresh, hot cookies. At Tower Records we'd mill around a while, then drive back to work. We thought it was great fun until we had to confess it to our boss who operated strictly by the book.

Sometime later in my career, when I was promoted to the position of supervisor and Ruth reported to me, I noticed she never took more than an hour for lunch, and sometimes not even that much. One day when we were chatting about "the old days" before I became her boss, I asked her why. I told her she was free to take more time if she wanted to because I knew how much she had enjoyed our little jaunts. Besides, she worked harder than anyone in the entire department did. She wasn't one to look a gift perk in the mouth.

Her answer makes my point about how grace and freedom work together: "I don't need to do it now, Luci . . . because I know I can." *I know I can.* Of course! When we've been liberated in Christ, he gives us the desire to do the right thing. As in any love relationship, as the love grows so does the desire to honor and please the loved one.

Unfortunately, one of the great hazards of our Christian culture is the legalism of other believers. Paul spoke to this directly. In essence, he teaches that as God's children we no longer have to meet others' demands that we be like them and abide by their rules, traditions, opinions, preferences. We are liberated by the spiritual reality that Christ has set us free to be who *he* wants us to be. Paul urges believers to stay away from the law forever: "So Christ has made us free. Now make sure that you stay free and don't get all tied up again in the chains of slavery" (Galatians 5:1 LB). A few verses later he adds, "Christ is useless to you if you are counting on clearing your debt to God by keeping those laws; you are lost from God's grace" (Galatians 5:4 LB).

In my view, our worst enemy today is not unbelief, but legalism. It is that thing in us that wants to tell everybody else what to do, how to live, when to respond, and where to enlist. That is not our right. Instead, we have the responsibility to extend the grace and love of Christ to others so they don't stay tangled up in the ropes of slavery. Hebrews 12:14–15 compels us: "Make every effort to live in peace with all men and to be holy; without holiness no one will see the Lord. See to it that no one misses the grace of God and that no bitter root grows up to cause trouble and defile many."

Legalism causes bitterness, trouble, and defilement. Some of us have lived in slavery to those things for so long, we don't even know it anymore. We just know we've fallen down and can't get up.

Look into your own heart and see if that is you. If so, ask the Lord to free you from that yoke of slavery and soar freely in his grace. That is your gift from God—as outrageous as it is. Christ set you free from everything and everybody so you could be a slave to him alone. And that's where the fun starts! With this kind of freedom you can walk the tightropes in your life with confidence, juggle your problems with assurance that he'll catch what gets out of alignment, clown around acting goofy because it's who you really are, and fly through the air with the greatest of ease because he'll catch you every time.

Try it. I think you'll agree it's the only way to live. Just remember to love God. Then doing as you please will please and glorify him. ☆

Sideshow

Freedom: A Christian's Comprehensive Guide
by BARBARA JOHNSON

"'Everything is permissible'—but not everything is beneficial. 'Everything is permissible'—but not everything is constructive. Nobody should seek his own good, but the good of others" (1 Corinthians 10:23–24). ☆

Chapter 14

Go for the Puddle

by MARILYN MEBERG

Mud puddles and little boys just seem to go together. (Remember Sheila's splashings of joy with her son Christian?) As my three-year-old grandson Ian and I trundled home from our ice cream break in downtown Carmel, California, Ian spotted a puddle made substantial from the periodic rain we'd been dodging all afternoon. Stopping for a moment, Ian eyeballed the puddle and then me. "Maungya, I think we should walk in it . . . whadaya think?"

Doing some eyeballing of my own, I noted his little canvas tennis shoes which could easily dry later as well as the fact we were only a block from home. Nevertheless, I decided to pass the buck. "What would Mama say?" I asked.

Thinking for a second Ian responded, "Are you my boss, Maungya?"

"No, your mama is."

Mulling this over briefly he said, "I think Mama says do it."

"Okay, you go first and I'll follow."

With wet shoes but lifted spirits we then continued our short trek for home.

"Do you have a boss, Maungya?" Ian asked as we sloshed along enjoying an even deeper sense of camaraderie than usual. Quickly evaluating whether I should launch into a discussion of personal responsibility to God, country, and job, I elected to keep it simple and said, "No, I don't really have a boss."

Stopping dead in his tracks, Ian stared up at me. "Well, who tells you what to do?"

"Basically no one," I answered.

"Wow," he sighed. "No boss."

The next morning, shortly before I was getting ready to leave Ian's house for the nine-hour drive to mine, he crawled into my lap, pulled my ear down to his mouth, and whispered, "I'm gonna try to find you a boss, Maungya."

"Really, Ian."

"Yeah, but don't tell Mama."

"Why shouldn't I tell Mama?"

"Well, 'cause she might wanna help and she's too busy."

I thanked him for wanting to include me in his life of servitude and giggled inwardly, wondering if he thought the reason Mama was so busy was because she was bossing him.

All of us, from our earliest days, know what yearning to be free from "bosses" feels like. That yearning may be as uncomplicated and easily gratified as wanting to splash in a puddle, stay in the sandbox after dark, or not return to the dorm room until 3 A.M. in spite of an 8 A.M. exam. On the other end of the spectrum, that yearning, when never satisfied, can deaden the human spirit beyond recognition.

The American poet Edwin Markham presents a wrenching image of that deadness in his poem "The Man with the Hoe."

> *Bowed by the weight of centuries he leans*
> *Upon his hoe and gazes on the ground.*
> *The emptiness of ages in his face*
> *And on his back the burden of the world.*
> *Who made him dead to rapture and despair,*
> *A thing that grieves not and never hopes,*
> *Stolid and stunned, a brother to the ox?*

Some of you may be muttering, "Good grief, Marilyn, you got kind of heavy all of a sudden! I don't feel like an ox, and I don't think I've ever stared at the ground with my chin propped up by a hoe!" But let me ask you, have you ever felt dead inside? Have you ever felt empty, even lifeless at times? I can tell you from my own experience, hoe or no hoe, that I have indeed felt empty . . . sometimes even lifeless. "But how could that be?" you might ask. "You're a Christian, filled with the Spirit of God. You're not supposed to feel empty and lifeless." True. But from time to time I lose the freedom God means for me to have in my relationship with him. When that happens, I begin to feel diminished—perhaps not "dead to rapture and despair," but diminished in my ability to fully respond to life as well as to God.

So what's wrong? After all, the prophet Isaiah called us forth from a place of servitude to a place of freedom: "He has sent me to bind up the brokenhearted, to proclaim freedom for the captives and release from darkness for the prisoners"

(Isaiah 61:1). Isaiah 49:9 invites "captives" to break out of their bondage: "'Come out,' and to those in darkness, 'Be free!'" And again in Isaiah 42:6–7: "I, the LORD, have called you in righteousness. . . . to open eyes that are blind, to free captives from prison and to release from the dungeon those who sit in darkness."

What incredible images: sitting in darkness, prisoners, captives, release. And surrounding those images is the liberating call to "come out" and to "be free!" We are called forth from the darkness to know him who is the light . . . Jesus. John 8:12 states, "I am the light of the world. Whoever follows me will never walk in darkness, but will have the light of life." And again in John 12:46 Jesus says, "I have come into the world as a light, so that no one who believes in me should stay in darkness."

I have been sprung from the darkness of prison to freedom with him who is the light. He means for me never to walk in darkness again. That should take care of it then; I should experience the freedom of any jailbird recently returned to outside society.

But you know what happens to me sometimes? I forget that I'm free. I forget that I've been called forth from the darkness, and because of that forgetting, I occasionally, though unwittingly, crawl back into my self-imposed prison. I sit there with the keys dangling in my hand because I've never fully comprehended or appropriated the words "be free!"

What does it mean to be free? Very simply (but so very profound in all its implications) I now live under grace instead of law. John 1:17 states clearly, "For the law was given through Moses; grace and truth came through Jesus Christ." That makes me free!

Free from what? Free from trying to be good enough to win God's favor, free from following rigid rules designed to produce good behavior, free from the guilt and shame stemming from impulses that keep reminding me I'm a mess, free from the pressure to perform perfectly, free to love myself in spite of myself, free to relax in his presence and even marvel that he actually enjoys me and isn't wondering why I'm not "doing something for him because the time is short," etc., etc. Jesus said in John 8:32, "You will know the truth, and the truth will set you free." The truth is that Christ set me free from the law by fulfilling the law on the cross. That means that what I do and how I serve him is not the ticket to my freedom, nor is it the means by which I impress him or win his love.

You might be tempted at this point to say, "Now, Marilyn honey, what you've just written is very basic to our walk with Christ. It seems odd that you don't appear to have a firm grasp of these primary truths. All believers know we live under grace and not under law!"

Let me respectfully whisper back, "Why, then, are so many of us hung up on our spiritual performance?" And I say "us" because I know I've got a lot of company out there in "Believer Land." We feel guilty that we haven't prayed enough, memorized or studied Scripture enough, witnessed enough, fasted and prayed enough, supported or adopted enough orphans, served on enough church committees, or baked enough cookies for shut-ins, and so on. These are the kinds of thoughts and emotions that cause us to turn from the Light. The next thing we know we're back in that dark place groping about for a candle. But to be free means we don't have to be anything or do anything. We can stop constantly evaluating ourselves.

I used to worry that if I took grace that literally, I'd quit working to further the kingdom of God. I feared that a relaxed acceptance of God's grace would encourage a slothful, lazy, maybe even indifferent approach to living that would land me in a hammock somewhere tossing berries in the air and counting the number that actually fell into my mouth. However, that has not been the case at all. Instead, I have found that grace so softens and moves my spirit, touches so deeply that core of gratitude within me, that I want to serve him. Law says I *have* to serve him; grace makes me *want* to serve him. I do so out of a heart of love.

But here's the part I have to watch out for in all this: If I start drifting from the position that I serve out of love because of God's grace and I slide imperceptibly toward being conscious of me, what I'm doing, how I'm doing it, and how much I'm doing, my focus shifts from the Light. When that happens I lose my freedom. Before long, it gets dark. I've imprisoned myself again.

What I hate about prison living is not only the darkness but the voices. (Uh oh, Marilyn's really gone over the edge now!) My cell echoes with feedback about my performance: "I know I should do better; I know I should do more; I know I should try harder." Or maybe, and here's a thought, "Someone else should do 'it'—someone more gifted or more spiritual." Good grief, by now I don't even want a candle! I just sit there crouched on my little camp stool with no memory of where those keys in my hand came from.

Why are so many of us prone to live our lives thinking we need to do more or be more? Some of it has to do with the parental messages we received as we were growing up. Those messages shape us, mold us, and more often than not, determine our behavior patterns and thought processes as adults. For example, if a child is rarely complimented, but only told to do better, he or she is likely to try throughout life to "get it right." The proverbial example is the child who's thrilled with her report card of all A's except for one B. If her parent's response is to ignore the A's and say only, "Let's get that B up to an A next time; looks like you need to work harder," that child may indeed "do better" but the message imprinted on her soul is, "Whatever I do, it's not enough; I need to do more."

I wouldn't be surprised if that experience was familiar to my doctor, who is considered to be one of the finest internists in the desert. She is a young woman who looks as if she might have graduated into the fourth grade sometime last spring. She's cute, energetic, appropriately thin, articulate, knowledgeable, and extremely well-groomed. For some reason, she always seems to annoy me slightly.

Several months ago my blood pressure was edging up a bit and she warned me that I might need to consider medication. I had a fit! I didn't want to take medication. The whole notion of having high blood pressure offended me! That was an old lady malady, I reasoned. And besides, I didn't want to start popping pills other than that little pink one that keeps me from growing facial hair and singing bass. Dr. "Precious" gave me six weeks to shape up.

Shape up I did! I cut out red meat and all butter (groan) from my diet. I began walking vigorously on the treadmill until I was doing an hour a day. In addition, I thought nothing but pleasant, charitable thoughts about myself, my neighbors, and the entire world!

At my next appointment, I was jubilant when my blood pressure read in the normal range. "Fantastic!" I fairly shouted to Dr. Precious. With that fixed, maddening little smile, she ignored my victory chant and asked how long it took me to walk a mile. "Twenty minutes." I grinned expectantly. With no altering of that insipid smile, she suggested I might, for the sake of my cardiovascular system, increase my speed until I could do a fifteen-minute mile. I wanted to leap from my chair and shout, "You tidy little twirp! The least you could do is congratulate me!" However, being the constrained and appropriate woman that I am, I wordlessly watched her straight little back disappear out the door to meet her next patient. I thought, "I'll bet growing up in your home was no picnic. You probably graduated from medical school with top honors at the age of twelve and no one in your family even mentioned it."

Not only do we need to consider why so many of us live enslaved to the "you can and should be doing more" philosophy, but we might also benefit from asking why is it so hard to accept, take in, and swallow down, the freedom that accompanies God's grace. I suppose one answer to that quandary is that no one, absolutely no one in our entire experience, loves us with no strings attached. No one is so thrilled with us, overjoyed to be with us, and wants nothing more than to express that love to us constantly, except God. But because that never happens to us on this earth, we can't quite grasp it. Is there a catch? Maybe it isn't really true.

Philip Yancey proclaims, "There's nothing I can do to make God love me more, and nothing I can do to make God love me less!" That means I can witness to 8,962 people before lunch tomorrow, lead them to Christ, supply them with follow-up material, and God will not be any more impressed with me or love me more than if I played golf instead, breaking my usual two or three windows along the way.

That means that even though I thought I was called to the mission field but got married instead and had four children, God still does not love me any more or any less even though I never went to Romania.

That means that even though I yell at my kids and hate myself for doing it, God still does not love me any more or any less in spite of my lack of self-control.

Even though I stood on a platform ministering to thousands, but because of my adulterous affairs, had to resign and leave behind hordes of disappointed, disillusioned people, God does not love me any less.

Can you wrap your mind around that kind of love? Do you find yourself saying a few "yeah, buts"? That kind of love is nothing short of outrageous. It defies human logic. It defies human experience.

I think one reason we so often stutter over his consistent love for us in spite of our performance is that we confuse his discipline with his love. For instance, the adulterous Christian leader who left thousands stunned and disillusioned is not going to experience any lessening of God's love. But he or she will have to realize that even though God's love never ceases, he does not condone sin. Because God loves that leader, God won't leave him or her to muck around in debauchery. God's intent is to raise all of us from that level of living.

And while the woman who felt called to the mission field but married instead has not diminished God's love for her, she may have diminished the degree and extent of the spiritual blessing that might have been hers. God will of course love and bless her in the life she has chosen, but she might always have a nebulous longing of her heart, especially when she sees pictures or hears stories about Romania.

The mother who yells at her children is much in need of parenting skills, impulse control, and self-discipline, but God does not love her less because she lacks those. But I'll bet you the three fat-free cookies in my pantry that somehow God will bring to her attention better ways to parent. Sometime, sooner or later, that mama is either going to read something or hear something that will cause her to question her parenting methods.

God intends to elevate us from the depths to which we can fall, but his discipline and the natural consequences he lets us experience are motivated by his love for us, not his condemnation of us. Because God is a good Father, because his love is pervasive and consistent, he will indeed discipline us when we need it, stretch us when we require it, and bring us to a level of maturity that is often very much against our inclinations. But in it all, he continues to love us and be pleased with us.

Our earthly experience is so different. We're used to people being pleased with us only when we get the job done—and even then, only when it's done well! But here's God, loving us in the midst of even our failure, but raising us up at the same time. That truth frees us from all the performance traps we will ever encounter and all the prisons we've ever sat in. The times in my life when I identify with the man with the hoe, I'm forgetting that God calls me forth from the prison of my self-effort and self-absorption. God, through his Son Jesus, sets me free from all that keeps me from living in the Light.

If you, like I, sometimes forget that God could not love you more, does not want you to be tormented by the echoes of those voices that say "more is not enough," that his plan for you is utter freedom and delight in knowing him and being loved by him, then join me in chanting our emancipation proclamation as stated in Galatians 5:1:

> *It is for freedom that Christ has set us free.*
> *Stand firm, then, and do not let yourselves be*
> *burdened again by a yoke of slavery.*

The words that struck the law-abiding religious folks of Jesus' day as outrageous are equally outrageous today. A holy King who could rule with an iron hand instead captivates through liberating his subjects. If that's not cause for celebration, I don't know what is!

If you're sitting in a prison cell, notice the keys dangling from your hand and consider who locked you in. It wasn't God. So come out! Be free! No one who believes in him should stay in darkness. Just ask my grandson Ian. Go for the puddle! ☆

Free Indeed!

by BARBARA JOHNSON

"Then you will know the truth, and the truth will set you free" (John 8:32).

And just what does the truth set us free *from?*

Accusation
Anguish
Blame
Bondage
Burdens
Fear
Guilt
Infirmities
Love of money
Oppression
Sin
Temptation
Traps

God's truth frees us "like a gazelle from the hand of the hunter, like a bird from the snare of the fowler" (Proverbs 6:5). His truth transforms us from being "prisoners [of] the waterless pit" to "prisoners of hope" (Zechariah 9:11–12).

Yet the Christian life is not a free-for-all; it comes with a road map. With the psalmist we sing, "I run in the path of your commands, for you have set my heart free" (Psalm 119:32).

"So if the Son sets you free, you will be free indeed" (John 8:36). ☆

Chapter 15

Swallowing Swords

by THELMA WELLS

The sword swallower's act at the circus entertains and amazes thousands, but please—do they really expect us to believe that anybody can get a sword past his tongue without cutting his throat out? There must be a spring or some kind of contraption to keep the blade from slicing through his vocal cords, not to mention his heart. But the illusion of it all is the thrilling part. We stand and gasp at this attraction, wondering how in the world he does it.

In real life, God calls us to swallow swords every day—the sharp blades of others' sin, unkindness, prejudice, injustice. I've heard people say, "I don't take nothing off nobody!" What a crock! We all "take stuff" every day—off our boss, our family, our neighbors, our government, our church members, our utility provider, our telephone company . . . oh, I don't have to continue with this, it could take all day. It's impossible to live in the real world without getting jabbed, cut, and sometimes seriously wounded by the swords that others wield.

It wasn't so long ago that I had to go around to the back door of a restaurant to order a hamburger, just because my skin wasn't white. And there I stood, next to the garbage dumpster in the alley, waiting for my order. It's tempting, isn't it, to flash our own weapons and fight evil with more evil. Luci already mentioned Saint Augustine's daring charge to believers: "Love God and do as you please." But sometimes what we "please" is to smack the person next to us for her unkind remark, his undeserved abuse, her annoying pettiness. No wonder Paul felt the need to remind us, "Do not use your freedom to indulge the sinful nature; rather, serve one another in love" (Galatians 5:13).

Jesus himself demanded something even more outrageous: "But I tell you who hear me: Love your enemies, do good to those who hate you, bless those who curse you, pray for those who mistreat you. If someone strikes you on one cheek, turn to him the other also. If someone takes your cloak, do not stop him from taking your tunic. Give to everyone who asks you, and if anyone takes what belongs to you, do not demand it back. Do to others as you would have them do to you" (Luke 6:27–31).

Say what! Does God really expect me to just "swallow it" when I'm mistreated? I don't want nobody slapping me around, and I certainly don't want to say, "Here, do it again on the other side. I want to be in the will of God!" But the apostle Paul explained, "For it is commendable if a man bears up under the pain of unjust suffering because he is conscious of God. But how is it to your credit if you receive a beating for doing wrong and endure it? But if you suffer for doing good and you endure it, this is commendable before God" (1 Peter 2:19–20).

When I had to drink out of a water fountain labeled "Colored" because I might contaminate the water for white folks, was that kind of outrageous injustice okay? Did God just want me and other black folks to take it? Dr. Martin Luther King, Jr., didn't think so. I don't think so. But one thing I have learned through the years: even while we're taking stuff off other people, we don't have to be hostile and hateful. We are free to hate; but as Christians, wouldn't it be more fitting to use our freedom to love?

In the mid-seventies I experienced something that I'd never experienced before or since. I was very involved in my church—singing in the choir and attending several services during the week. I enjoyed the Sunday afternoon teas and other church socials, and relished the Christian fellowship. For some reason unknown to me, however, one of the older ladies at church decided that she did not like me one bit. She had known me since I was four years old and she'd watched me graduate from college, marry and become a mother, begin my career in banking. For years we had held pleasant conversations and never had a conflict.

Then, quite suddenly, she became distant from me. When I spoke to her she'd look at me with disdain, but give no verbal response. It got so bad that when I would walk into a room where she was, she would demonstrate her hatred for me by saying something catty about me to someone else and then leaving the room. Even while we were in the choir room or seated in the choir stand, she would make it known through her words or facial expressions and body language that I was the object of her distaste.

Perplexed, embarrassed, frustrated, and hurt at how she treated me, I tried to approach her to ask her if I had done or said anything that would cause her to turn on me like a vicious dog. She refused to give me the time of day. I surfed through my mind and searched my soul to see if I had talked negatively about her to anybody, if I had spoken to her unkindly. I wracked my brain for any possibility of error on my part that would make her treat me so poorly. I prayed and asked God to reveal to me what this was all about. Nothing! I knew of nothing to explain her behavior.

As the months passed, the situation did not improve. For two years I continued to pray with her and the rest of the choir before services, worship with her in church, attend functions she attended, and receive the same unfair, mean, embarrassing treatment. Sometimes I couldn't make it to my car fast enough before the tears would stream down my face because I was so hurt and confused over the situation. It was like a sword that had pierced my heart, leaving me bleeding on the inside.

Naturally, I thought seriously about being ugly to her. I even rehearsed in my mind what I would say or do to punish her for her meanness. But I also prayed—hard! I knew from God's Word that I had a choice about how to respond. I knew I could use my freedom to hate or to love. God himself showed me how to choose love: "When someone gives you a hard time, respond with the energies of prayer, for then you are working out of your true selves, your God-created selves. This is what God does. He gives his best—the sun to warm and the rain to nourish—to everyone, regardless: the good and bad, the nice and nasty" (Matthew 5:4–45 THE MESSAGE).

By the power of the Holy Spirit, I chose to give my best. Never did I stop speaking, smiling, and attempting to communicate with this friend who had become my enemy. Week after week, month after month, I prayed that I would not stoop to her level—that I would not be overcome by anger, bitterness, and the desire for revenge.

Was it easy to keep from falling into those natural emotional traps? No! If I'd depended solely on myself to take the high road, I would never have made it. But I had faith enough to believe that God would give me everything it took to swallow that sword without spilling blood.

Over time my prayers changed from "God, please show me what I've done to her" to "God, since I haven't done anything to deserve this treatment, please soften her heart toward me. Prompt her to come to me and tell me she's sorry. Then I will be vindicated, she will be delivered, we can be reconciled, and you will be glorified."

Finally, one Sunday morning I was asked to pray during our choir's devotional time prior to entering the sanctuary for worship. When I finished praying, lo and behold, my enemy walked straight over to me, bent and broken, tears flooding her eyes. Wrapping her arms around my shoulders and laying her head on my neck, she said with a repentant spirit, "Thelma baby, I'm sooo sorry. Please forgive me. Please forgive me. I'm so sorry. I cannot keep this up any longer. Please forgive me."

The tears of sorrow I had shed over this situation turned to tears of rejoicing! As our teardrops streamed together, the sword of this experience sprung out of my heart and my

wounds were healed. The grace of God that had been flow-
ing through me for nearly three years because of fervent
prayer and reliance on the Holy Spirit enabled me to accept
the apology of this woman who had betrayed and hurt me.
We briefly whispered a prayer of thanksgiving together and
proceeded to go to the sanctuary for a time of worship that
was sweeter than either of us had known during our years of
estrangement.

If I had stopped speaking to this woman and treated her
badly because she treated me that way, things would not
have turned out the way they did. You see, God honors our
obedience to his Word, even when it doesn't make sense to
us or we find it as difficult as swallowing a sword. When
Jesus told us to turn the other cheek, he wasn't talking about
letting someone literally beat on us. Rather, he was referring
to one of the spiritual principles that turns everything on its
head and changes the world: loving one's enemies. "'If your
enemy is hungry, feed him; if he is thirsty, give him something to drink. In doing this, you will heap burning coals on
his head.' Do not be overcome by evil, but overcome evil
with good" (Romans 12:20–21).

Every day at work, home, school, and play, God presents
us with opportunities to be a blessing to people who may not
be as nice to us as we deserve or desire. In the middle of
these opportunities he strengthens us and enables us to pay
back good for evil. It may be as small as giving a genuinely
friendly smile to someone who's been ugly to you.

It may be complimenting someone who is obviously jeal-
ous of you. It may be graciously offering to ease a colleague's
workload even though she never offers to help you. Instead of
giving those who mistreat you a taste of their own medicine,

bless them. Pray for them. Be ready to come to their aid if they need you. Forgive them. Show them the love of Jesus.

Talk about swallowing swords! How in the world can we do it? I have discovered that God never tells us to do anything that is impossible to do. What he says may not make complete sense to us, but it is good sense to do it anyway. In his graciousness he has given us the freedom to make choices, the ability to think for ourselves. But he has also given us a rule book, a procedures manual to guide our conduct. The great thing about the Author of that book is that he teaches by example.

There is no greater expert on the subject of swallowing swords than the Son of God. Because Jesus was born in a barn, lived the humble life of a carpenter's son, was ridiculed in the synagogue, kicked out of his own town, stalked by the curious and the government, betrayed by one of his disciples, and died by crucifixion, he knows firsthand everything we feel when we swallow the sharp swords of life. And he is the only perfect example of how to act. "To this you were called, because Christ suffered for you, leaving you an example, that you should follow in his steps. 'He committed no sin, and no deceit was found in his mouth.' When they hurled their insults at him, he did not retaliate; when he suffered, he made no threats. Instead, he entrusted himself to him who judges justly" (1 Peter 2:21–23).

Do you remember when Jesus was rejected in his own hometown? In Luke 4, Jesus had just spent forty days successfully resisting Satan's snares in the desert, and he'd come back to civilization drenched in the power of the Holy Spirit. After preaching in Galilee, news about him spread throughout the countryside. When he came home to Nazareth where he'd been raised, everyone at the synagogue was impressed with his celebrity and no doubt wanted to see him "do his stuff" among his own.

But Jesus wasn't impressed with his townspeople's spiritual blindness. They still couldn't recognize him for who he was; they couldn't get beyond the fact that he was just a homegrown boy. "Isn't this Joseph's son?" they asked. They couldn't accept that the hometown hero was the Son of God. Jesus condemned them for their shortsightedness and let them know in no uncertain terms that, just as in Elijah's time, God's glory would continue to be revealed in spite of them. God wanted Jesus to take the message of the kingdom to the Gentiles, and that's exactly what he would do.

The people were enraged that Joseph's son would rebuke them; who did he think he was? So they drove him out of town and took him to the brow of a cliff with the intent to throw him off. Jesus could have fought them. He could have opened the ground to swallow them up. He could have turned them into blades of grass or hay to feed the cattle. He could have killed their children and separated them from their spouses. But he didn't do any of those dramatic things. Instead, he swallowed the sword of rejection and simply continued on his way—right through the hostile crowd to the next town where the people were ripe for his message.

Never in the pages of Jesus' life can we find that he fought back with the human techniques we attempt to use. Instead, he endured stuff to demonstrate his love and to show us how to swallow the swords that come at us. Even in his final moments of agony Jesus showed humanity what it means to use one's freedom to serve in love. He could have leapt down off the cross and slaughtered his oppressors, but

instead he freely gave up his life in order to save the very
ones who hated him. Instead of hurling invectives as he
died, he prayed for his enemies: "Father, forgive them, for
they do not know what they are doing" (Luke 23:34).

In this human realm, none of that makes any sense. It's
outrageous! But God has given us every resource we need to
be able to do the humanly senseless with heavenly sense.
When we ask God to take away anything in us that would
keep us from doing his perfect will, we can be liberated to
love our enemies and do all kinds of outrageous things like
Jesus did. Jesus said, "So if the Son sets you free, you will be
free indeed" (John 8:36). As followers of the Son, we are
freed from the power of sin. When we are tempted to wield
our own sword against someone who's wronged us, the Holy
Spirit within us prompts us to do the right thing . . . forgive
and pray for our enemy. The Spirit within us acts as a spring
in the sword of life so that when we are attacked, we can
swallow the sword without cutting our heart out. If we are
children of God and joint heirs with Jesus, we have the
attributes of our spiritual relatives—enough love, understanding, forgiveness, power, and grace to be able to swallow
the swords of life without getting bloody.

You can do it. You can treat your enemies with love and
respect even as they mistreat you. You can love your neighbors as you love yourself, even if they throw trash in your
yard and yell at your children. You can forgive the ugly things
people have done and said to you, and pardon them as God
has pardoned you. No, it's not easy. But the practice of perfect
makes perfect. Start practicing today by asking God to
remove all the blocks that have kept you from forgiving and
loving people. Talk to a Christian friend who will listen to

your hurts and give you Scripture-based advice on how to respond. Most important, follow the example of Jesus, "the author and perfecter of our faith, who for the joy set before him endured the cross, scorning its shame, and sat down at the right hand of the throne of God" (Hebrews 12:2). ☆

The First Stone
by Barbara Johnson

For years I've carried a little rock in my luggage everywhere I go. It's been my handy ammunition, a missile to throw at those who make mistakes. It's not a big stone—nothing that would cause brain damage. It's just a smooth, round stone about the size of my fist, perfect for delivering a timely jolt of condemnation. To be honest, I've considered throwing that old rock away; after all, it adds extra weight to my luggage. But I never know when I might need it.

My daughter-in-love, Shannon, decided I'd carried my rock around for so long that it needed a bit of sprucing up. On one side of it she painted a little picture of two lambs grazing in the valley (because, as Shannon says, that's where the fertilizer is, so that's where we grow). Then she stuck it back in my suitcase.

The next time I was traveling and someone was nasty to me, I dug through my bag, looking for the rock. *Boy, I'm really gonna do it this time!* I fumed. The rock felt smooth and hard in my hand. Then I noticed the picture of the little lambs and the words Shannon had painted under the scene: "Barb's first stone. John 8:7." The rock went back into my luggage.

I continue to carry that little rock with me everywhere I travel, but now it's not ammo; it's God's gracious reminder that I have a choice about how to respond to those who mistreat me. God has given me outrageous freedom; I'm free at any time to hurl stones of condemnation at the sinners around me ... just as soon as I become sinless myself.

☆
Afterword

The Greatest Show on Earth

by PATSY CLAIRMONT

Luci is such an enthusiast for life that her buoyancy over even the simplest of things is highly contagious. We, as her friends, know that she loves hot air balloons, not only for the aerial ride they offer, but also for the photo op they provide as they float overhead. So whenever we see one, we all alert Luci, who then appears with her super-duper camera and clicks endless frames of these nomadic airships.

When we were in Albuquerque, New Mexico, for a Women of Faith conference, we knew we were in balloon country, so we had our eyes to the sky. Mary Graham, Luci's roommate and the whole staff's best friend as well as the conference's emcee, is an early riser. On our first morning in Albuquerque, she spotted a formation of balloons drifting over the mountain range. Of course, she and Luci were joyous. Well, when I heard of their sighting I was both excited and disappointed, for I, too, wanted to see these delicate bubbles waltz in the wind. So my roomie, Lana, and I became more attentive to the horizon in hopes of an appearance.

The next morning Mary announced that she and Luci had seen half a dozen more balloons at sunrise. Lana and I saw nothing. Since I am more a sundown person, I began to wonder if I'd have to change my ways if I wanted to have a glimpse of these colorful sky-wonders. But on our last day in

212 AFTERWORD—Outrageous Joy

New Mexico, as I was dressing, Lana called to me, "Patsy, come quick! Balloons! Balloons!"

I bolted out of the bathroom and across the room to the window. It took a moment to focus, but sure enough, there they were: six red balloons whose strings had slipped from a child's hand on the sidewalk below. I whirled around only to find Lana snickering into her suitcase. What a clown! I turned back to the window and watched as the tiny circus bouquet skipped merrily away.

No, I never did see a billowing balloon wandering the sky in search of a view, at least not on that trip; but since then I've thought of the importance of looking up during our journey on earth. Our time is short, and eternity is just over the mountain range. I've noticed that those who purpose to be sunrise (joyful) people experience some of the best views.

Joy is like a bouquet of balloons from Jesus meant to hearten us. Not the circus kind that float willy-nilly, but the hot air kind that have a predetermined direction. I believe we enter into our joy as we determine to tilt our hearts upward, for an upward tilt allows us to receive all he has to offer.

The outrageous women I work with are some of the most joyful women I have ever known. And you can always detect the difference between joy and happiness. Too much happiness in a person is like too much cotton candy—sugary, sticky, and a little nauseating. Whereas joy is like a hot air balloon, for it lifts all who enter it, it buoys the spirit, and it offers a higher perspective.

The view for a woman of joy is one of expectancy and hope. Like Barbara, who has been an example of joy despite circumstances. And Marilyn, who reminds me that joy is often a choice. And Luci, who demonstrates that joy is everywhere. And Thelma, who is a wellspring of joy. (Honey, you can't give it away if you don't have it.) And Sheila, whose life portrays the "full and running over" kind of joy that others want to splash around in.

At our conferences Thelma sings, "I've got the joy, joy, joy, joy down in my heart." If you sang this song in Sunday school, you know that the question is then sung out, "Where?" and the response is an affirmative "Down in my heart!" Why? To remind us that this is an inside job between the Lord and us. He gives us joy, and then we choose to respond out of it. Which takes us back to the tilt of our heart. The more receptive we are to the Lord, the more likely we are to have the joy, joy, joy, joy, way down in the depths of our heart.

When joy is deep within us, we will walk through this life with a lifted heart, soul, and mind. Then one day, one outrageous day, we will see on the horizon the Son rise. This, friends, will be more stunning, more thrilling, more exhilarating than a New Mexico sky teeming with hot air balloons. So be attentive, keep your eye on the sky, your feet on the ground, and your heart tilted heavenward. Until then, enjoy the view. It's the greatest show on earth! ☆

WOMEN OF FAITH℠

1999 Conference Schedule

May 7-8....................Kansas City, MO
June 11-12.........................Detroit, MI
June 18-19.................Cleveland, OH
June 25-26......................Orlando, FL
July 9-10.........................Houston, TX
July 16-17.............E. Rutherford, NJ
July 23-24.......................Atlanta, GA
July 30-31.........................Chicago, IL
August 6-7................Indianapolis, IN
August 20-21.................Seattle, WA
August 27-28....................Dallas, TX
September 10-11..........Anaheim, CA
September 17-18............Denver, CO
September 24-25........Pittsburgh, PA
October 1-2................Richmond, VA
October 15-16.............Charlotte, NC
October 29-30........Minneapolis, MN

2000 Conference Schedule

January 28-29............Cincinnati, OH
February 18-19......Washington, D.C.
March 3-4.....................SanDiego, CA
March 17-18...................San Jose, CA
April 7-8.........................Houston, TX
May 19-20......................Orlando, FL
June 16-17.......................Omaha, NE
July 14-15...........................Dallas, TX
July 21-22....................Memphis, TN
July 28-29.........................Buffalo, NY
August 11-12..................Chicago, IL
August 18-19................St. Louis, MO
August 25-26................Tacoma, WA
September 8-9..............Anaheim, CA
September 15-16...........Phoenix, AZ
September 29-30......Philadelphia, PA
October 27-28............Charlotte, NC
Date TBD.........................Atlanta, GA
Date TBD.........................Denver, CO
Date TBD................Minneapolis, MN

WOMEN OF FAITH℠

Outrageous Joy
is based on the popular
Women of Faith conferences.

Women of Faith is partnering with Zondervan Publishing House,
Integrity Music, *Today's Christian Woman* magazine, World Vision,
and Campus Crusade to offer conferences, publications, worship
music, and inspirational gifts that support and encourage today's
Christian women.

Since their beginning in January of 1996, the Women of Faith
conferences have enjoyed an enthusiastic welcome by women
across the country.

**Call 1-888-49-FAITH for the many conference
locations and dates available.**

Women of Faith Friends

Friends Through Thick & Thin

**Gloria Gaither,
Peggy Benson,
Sue Buchanan,
and Joy MacKenzie**

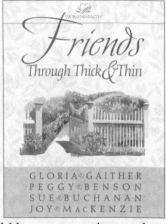

The authors, who have been good friends for over thirty years, celebrate the ups and downs and all-arounds of friendship. *Friends Through Thick & Thin* spotlights the relationships that add beauty, meaning, and sanity to our daily lives. Sit back and revel in this joyous, personal time of sharing with four extraordinary women.

Hardcover 0-310-21726-1
Softcover 0-310-22913-8

Deeper Joy for Your Journey

Bring Back the Joy
Sheila Walsh

Capturing the theme of the 1998 Women of Faith conferences, *Bring Back the Joy* is a warm, encouraging, and richly personal invitation to experience the joy that comes from loving and being loved by the Most Important Person in the universe. In *Bring Back the Joy*, Sheila Walsh writes about rekindling the joy in your life and in your relationship with God. With great wisdom gained through learning and growing with other women as a key speaker at Women of Faith conferences across the nation, she calls us to a deeper joy, exposes the negative forces designed to steal our joy, and shows us how to sow life-changing seeds of joy.

Hardcover 0-310-22023-8
Softcover 0-310-22915-4
Audio Pages 0-310-22222-2

More for Your Joyful Journey . . .

The Joyful Journey

**Patsy Clairmont,
Barbara Johnson,
Marilyn Meberg,
and Luci Swindoll**

With trademark warmth and good humor, the authors share from their hearts and lives about the obstacles, bumps, and detours we sometimes face along the journey of life and about how friendship, laughter, and celebration can help steer our hearts closer to God.

**Softcover 0-310-22155-2
Audio Pages 0-310-21454-8**

Devotions for Women of Faith

Joy Breaks

**Patsy Clairmont,
Barbara Johnson,
Marilyn Meberg,
and Luci Swindoll**

Ninety upbeat devotionals that motivate and support women who want to renew and deepen their spiritual commitment. These devotions illustrate practical ways to deepen joy amidst all the complexities, contradictions, and challenges of being a woman today. Women of all ages will be reminded that any time, any day, they can lighten up, get perspective, laugh, and cast all their cares on the One who cares for them.

Hardcover 0-310-21345-2

Joy Breaks Daybreak™

Bring joy to your life every day with 128 light-hearted, inspiring, and joyful devotional excerpts from the book *Joy Breaks*.

0-310-97287-6

Joy Given Is Joy Returned...and More!

Boomerang Joy

Barbara Johnson

In her first-ever devotional Barbara Johnson dares you to lighten up and enjoy life to the hilt. She writes, "You've got to hone your ability to fling a smile a mile. Sure as anything, it'll boomerang right back to you, more accurately each time you toss it out."

Barbara knows life is far too serious and too short not to laugh. In 60 wise, witty devotions—salted with humor and peppered with the madcap illustrations of syndicated cartoonist John McPherson—she encourages you to develop a joy-filled lifestyle. The perfect tonic for when you feel tired or worn out, or when you just need a good laugh and some heartfelt encouragement.

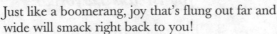

Just like a boomerang, joy that's flung out far and wide will smack right back to you!

Also available are a Boomerang Joy Daybreak™ perpetual calendar, a journal for writing all your thoughts and joyful prayers, and audio pages of the book.

Hardcover 0-310-22006-8
Softcover 0-310-23199-X
Audio Pages 0-310-22548-5
Daybreak 0-310-97707-X
Journal 0-310-97708-8

We want to hear from you. Please send your comments about this
book to us in care of the address below. Thank you.

ZondervanPublishingHouse

Grand Rapids, Michigan 49530

http://www.zondervan.com